W9-ARL-347

Teachers— Their World and Their Work

Implications for School Improvement

ANN LIEBERMAN AND LYNNE MILLER

TEACHERS COLLEGE PRESS

Teachers College, Columbia University
New York and London

Published by Teachers College Press, 1234 Amsterdam Avenue
New York, NY 10027

Copyright © 1992 by Teachers College, Columbia University

All rights reserved. No part of this publication may be reproduced or transmitted in any form or by any means, electronic or mechanical, including
photocopy, or any information storage and retrieval system, without permission from the publisher.

Library of Congress Cataloging-in-Publication Data

Lieberman, Ann.
    Teachers—their world and their work : implications for school
improvement / Ann Lieberman and Lynne Miller.
        p.   cm.
    Includes bibliographical references and index.
    ISBN 0–8077–3165–X
    1. Teaching.   2. Public schools—United States.   3. School
improvement programs—United States.   I. Miller, Lynne. 1945–
II. Title.
    LB1025.3.L54   1992
    371.1'02—dc20   91-32634
                                                           CIP

ISBN 0–8077–3165–X (pbk.)

Printed on acid-free paper
Manufactured in the United States of America

99 98 97 96 95 94   8 7 6 5 4 3 2

Contents

Theory is all grey
and the
golden tree of life
is green.

—*Goethe*

Introduction

This book first appeared in 1984, a propitious time for a discussion of school improvement. *A Nation at Risk* had appeared the previous year and the Carnegie Task Force's *A Nation Prepared* was in press. Though our own work was conceived and written well before the publication of these two national studies, we were influenced by the same conditions and social forces affecting other educators and critics writing at the time. Those years were marked by a growing doubt in America's ability to fulfill its promise, both as a major competitor in international markets and as an exemplar of democratic principles and practices. There were diverse and contradictory responses to this crisis of confidence, and many of the responses focused on the nation's public schools.

The author of the federally sponsored *A Nation at Risk* saw the schools as the training ground for the next generation of entrepreneurs and workers. They focused on improving student achievement and called for immediate and forceful policy directives on the part of the government. Supported by their state bureaucracies of education, elected officials were quick to mandate more courses, more tests, more standards, more requirements, more control. The message conveyed by *A Nation at Risk* was clear: Schools are responsible for the decline of the nation. The solution is for schools to redouble their energies, to—in effect—do the same thing harder.

The Carnegie Task Force responded in quite a different way. These writers' ultimate goals for schooling were less explicit and less instrumental. Though they hinted at a wider perspective on what schools are for, their focus was not on student outcomes, but on the social world of the schools, particularly the way the role of teacher had come to be defined. They argued for a new professionalism, for the creation of new roles within the teaching ranks, and for the development of teacher-initiated reforms. They supported a national standards board to certify master teachers and promoted a critical examination of how schools were structured as adult work environments. While they presented powerful insights about the nature of teaching and provided a clear focus for its professionalization, Task Force members were less clear about how changes in adult working conditions would translate into better education and enhanced achievement for students. The message conveyed was: Change the teacher role, professionalize the career, and the rest of schooling will change as well.

Our book provided yet another perspective, though our view was clearly more sympathetic to the Carnegie report. We were interested in exploring the connection between the conditions of teaching and learning. We relied more on description than on prescriptions, taking to heart Waller's advice that "whatever contributes to understanding also contributes to reconstruction" (1967). Our major goal was to derive meaning from "the field"—available conceptions, research, and experience, however tentative—and to develop an understanding of the social world of teaching from the teacher's perspective. Such understandings, we believed, would provide the foundation for action. It was our strong position, and our chief motive for writing, that teachers possessed the major portion of available knowledge about teaching and learning, and that it was only through a recognition of that knowledge and an articulation and understanding of it that educators and policy-makers could begin to find ways to improve schools. We operated on a strong hunch, informed by research and practice, that when we listened to the words of teachers and saw the world as they saw it, we would uncover some of what schools needed for their own regeneration.

We believe that our hypothesis about how schools change is still correct and worth reiterating. As we enter the 1990s, a new reform movement is in the making. The "restructuring" movement is, for us, a powerful and significant force in education; its mission is the reconceptualization and redesign of public schools. It acknowledges that schools are socializing agents for both the workplace and for productive citizenship in a democracy, as well as being places where children "learn to use their minds well" (Sizer, 1964). It recognizes that basic change in the content and process of schooling is necessary, and it challenges educators to assess critically the structures of schooling and the extent to which they inhibit or advance learning. Restructuring pushes educators to take action, to use the knowledge they accumulate in order to transform schools for the benefit of both students and teachers. Restructuring, in these terms, places teachers at the center of the reform enterprise.

In 1984, we argued that teachers, their world, and their work, were the cornerstones of educational change. We offered a perspective on schooling that challenged traditional notions and viewpoints. Rather than seeing schools "from the outside looking in," we wanted to develop understandings "from the inside out," and to encourge and convince others to join us. As the movement to restructure schools grows, we think it is appropriate to be reminded of the centrality of teachers and teaching in any improvement effort.

The sources for this book are many and varied. We have used field-notes from formal observations. We also depended on teacher logs, the professional literature on school reform, long-term ethnographics, and interviews. In addition, we relied on our own experiences, reflections, formulations, and reformulations about life in schools. We admit, up front, that we have been selective. We have deliberately sought specific examples and quotations that seem to represent general principles and understandings that provide a framework for action.

As writers, we want to be honest about the difficulties we faced in presenting an accurate and fresh view of teaching. We were continually made aware of the tension that exists between being good researchers and good practitioners. We had to protect against producing dry, "academic" writing and we had to guard against the allure of doing anecdotal reporting, of becoming so involved in the "nitty gritty" of our work in schools so as to suspend our critical faculties. The position we finally assumed is located along a continuum, with obscurantism at one pole and myopic familiarity at the other.

We are very pleased that Teachers College Press is reissuing this book at the present time. We believe quite strongly that **Teachers— Their World and Their Work** provides a useful framework for viewing and understanding schools. It also serves as a springboard for discussion about how to restructure schools and in what direction. We are in the process of writing a companion book to this volume, to be published by Teachers College Press, which focuses more directly on the current reform movement and how teachers are working to restructure their world and their work.

ANN LIEBERMAN
LYNNE MILLER
1992

References

Sizer, Ted. *Horace's Compromise*. Boston: Houghton-Mifflin, 1964.
Waller, Willard. *The Sociology of Teaching*. New York: John Wiley & Sons, 1967.

Acknowledgments

We are no different from other authors who, after they have finished a book, can't believe it is really completed. And like others, we recognize that what is in the pages is a sum total of much experience, discussion, care, and time. The ideas are ours, but they are clearly informed by the teachers who worked with us, let us into their classrooms, and helped us understand better what life is like from 7:45 to 3:30. Thanks to Flo and Janey and to all the teachers at the various high schools we visited.

Our colleagues at Teachers College and in the South Bend Community School Corporation have been especially helpful and supportive to us over the past four years. Thanks to Sally McConnell, who typed our manuscript with her usual efficiency and skill and developed an ownership in our work that sometimes equaled our own. And thanks also to Jim Ashley, who provided much-welcomed editorial assistance and objective criticism in the late stage of our writing.

To our husbands we owe a special thanks. They asked us tough questions and many times encouraged us to go back and clarify our thinking. They have heard us talk for years about our ideas and views of schools and teachers; throughout, they have shared our vision of working with teachers to develop opportunities for growth that nurture caring and concern, growth and development. Thanks to Ernie and Larry.

Not too many people get opportunities to collaborate under conditions of constant stimulation, creativity, and learning. For the most part, writing is a lonely job; we are lucky. We were able to cooperate, critique others' work even as we protected our own words, and come to a shared understanding of what we were doing. We were each other's best teacher, student, and friend throughout the process of writing together.

1

The Social Realities of Teaching

Whatever contributes to understanding also contributes to reconstruction.

—Willard Waller, 1967

In this first chapter, we develop a set of understandings about the nature of teaching and explore themes that capture some of the dailiness of working in schools. Our intention here is twofold: to begin to describe, in a general sense, what it is like to be a teacher, and to lay the groundwork for the chapters that follow, which dig more deeply into the specifics of life in elementary and secondary schools and which draw implications for the improvement of schooling on all levels.

The Nature of Teaching

We begin our discussion with a set of understandings about the nature of teaching as a profession. We have developed these understandings over time; they are based on the literature, current research, our work with teachers, and reflections on our own experiences. We label the set of phenomena we are about to describe as "social system understandings" because they reflect the interplay between individual teacher experiences and the social context of schools. These understandings serve as a basis for discussing generalizations about the way teachers

1

learn their jobs, become teachers, and forge a professional identity.

Style is Personalized

Teachers are faced with a central contradiction in their work, a contradiction that makes it incumbent upon each one of them to develop a style that is individual and personal. The contradiction stated simply is this: teachers have to deal with a group of students and teach them something and, at the same time, deal with each child as an individual. The teachers, then, have two missions: one universal and cognitive, and the other particular and affective. The cognitive mission demands a repertoire of skills in moving a group and making sure that knowledge builds, extends, and is learned. The affective mission requires that teachers somehow make friends with their students, motivate them, arouse their interest, and engage them on a personal level. In order to deal with this contradiction, teachers develop all kinds of strategies and then meld them together into a style that is highly personal, if not plain idiosyncratic. This style, forged in the dailiness of work developed from trial and error, becomes one's professional identity and, as such, may be militantly protected and defended.

Rewards are Derived from Students

The greatest satisfaction for a teacher is the feeling of being rewarded by one's students. In fact, most of the time the students are the *only* source of rewards for most teachers. Isolated in their own classrooms, teachers receive feedback for their efforts from the words, expressions, behaviors, and suggestions of the students. By doing well on a test, sharing a confidence, performing a task, indicating an interest, and reporting the effects of a teacher's influence, students let teachers know that they are doing a good job and are appreciated. Unlike other professionals who look to colleagues and supervisors for such feedback, teachers can only turn to children.

Teaching and Learning Links are Uncertain

Dan Lortie (1965) has said that teaching is fraught with "endemic uncertainties." No uncertainty is greater than the one that surrounds the connection between teaching and learning. A teacher does his or her best, develops curricula, tries new approaches, works with individuals and groups, and yet never knows for sure what are the effects. One hopes the children will get it, but one is never sure. A teacher operates out of a kind of blind faith that with enough in the way of planning, rational schemes, objectives, and learning activities some learning will take place. But a teacher also knows that some learnings happen that are significant and never planned for and that other learnings never take hold, despite the best of professional intentions.

The Knowledge Base is Weak

Throughout their careers, teachers seek professional knowledge. In preparation, a teacher-to-be takes numerous courses in the theory and the practice of education—most of which are judged as irrelevant upon entering teaching. As a bonafide teacher, one takes even more courses to earn permanent certification. In addition there is a plethora of "staff development" offerings made available and often mandated on the district level. With some exceptions, this inservice work is given the same low grades for relevance and helpfulness as is early pre-professional preparation. The sad fact is that, as a profession, we have not been able to codify teaching under a variety of contingencies in a way that is satisfying to practitioners. The knowledge base in teaching is weak; there is simply no consensus (as there is in medicine and law) about what is basic to the practice of the profession.

Goals are Vague and Conflicting

Although there is much talk of late about goal specificity and accountability, it is still the case that the goals of education are vague and often in conflict. Are we out to impart basic skills or to enrich lives? Do we concentrate on the individual or concern ourselves with the development of the group? Are we teaching to minimal levels of competence, or are we working to develop a wide range of talents and possibilities? Do we most value discipline or learning, order and control or intellectual curiosity? Are we socializing students, or are we educating them? The answer to these questions and to others like them is usually, "Yes, we are doing both." The result is that individual teachers make their own translations of policy and that, in general, the profession is riddled by vagueness and conflict.

Control Norms are Necessary

Daily teachers make an assault on gaining some sense of direction, control, and movement of their classes. Teachers work hard to develop a set of norms and rules that both they and their students can live with. This happens as teachers move through a cycle of giving orders, threatening, being tested, and finally reaching some standards that are accepted and move the class along. While this is being carried out in individual classrooms, schoolwide norms are also being tried and established. The setting of control norms is a necessary part of teaching; it satisfies the need for certainty in an otherwise ambiguous and uncertain world. It also assures teachers of their place in the organization of the school. No matter how effective teachers are in the classroom, all that is ever really known about them in the general organization of the school is whether they keep their classes in line or whether the students are in control. Control precedes instruction; this is a major shibboleth of teaching.

Professional Support is Lacking

Seymour Sarason has written that "Teaching is a Lonely Profession" (1966), a characterization that is indeed apt. Unlike other professions, teaching does not provide for a shared culture based on the movement from knowledge to experience in the company of one's peers. Doctors, for instance, learn their profession through a graduated set of experiences, all shared with others. Not so the teacher. Once graduated from a preparation program, teachers find themselves alone in the classroom with a group of students without a peer or supervisor in sight. The neophyte teacher is left with degree in hand, high expectations internalized, a fistful of untried methodologies, and few adults with whom to share, grow, and learn.

Teaching is an Art

Teaching is an art, despite current efforts to scientize it. Some parts of teaching may lend themselves to programming and rationalization, but in the long haul more artistry than science or technology is practiced as teachers struggle to adjust and readjust, to make routines, and establish patterns, only to recast what has been done in a new form to meet a new need or a new vision. Teachers are best viewed as craftspeople; the reality of teaching is of a craft learned on the job. This understanding is perhaps our most important; that is why we saved it for last. When viewed as a craft, teaching makes sense as a messy and highly personal enterprise, for it concerns itself with the making and remaking of an object until it satisfies the standards of its creator.

In codifying what we have called the "social system understandings" of teaching, we have attempted to impose some order on what is admittedly a disorderly landscape. As we do this, we are well aware that generalizations—no matter how grounded in the realities of practice—somehow always "miss the mark." While useful as guidelines for discussion about our craft, they fail to capture the flesh and blood of teaching, to call up its dailiness. In the section that follows we try to capture some of that dailiness as it is experienced by public school teachers and to build on some of the understandings we have presented here.

The Dailiness of Teaching

In this section, we move from understandings to themes. Specifically, we explore notions of *rhythms, rules, interactions,* and *feelings* as they are played out in the day-to-day work of teachers in public schools.

Rhythms

A teacher's professional life is measured in terms of years of service. Each of those years is cyclical, mediated by the rhythms of days, of weeks, of months, and of seasons. Let's begin by talking about teachers' days. Days begin early, before the din of the rush hour has peaked, often before the sun has risen. Once sign-in procedures are completed, greetings exchanged with colleagues, the last sip of coffee downed in the teachers' room, and the warning bell sounded, the classroom becomes a teacher's total world. It is a world that is unique and separate from the world of other adults. For six hours a day, five days a week, teachers live in an exclusive and totally controlled environment. For the majority of the day they are bound in space and time. In most instances, teachers need the permission of the principal to leave the building during school hours.

> *"Whoever heard of a profession where you can't even go to the bathroom when you have to?"*

Each day has its rhythm. For elementary teachers, the lunch hour divides the day into morning and afternoon activities, each marked by a recess and perhaps some instructional time with an itinerant teacher.

They may spend an entire day in one classroom with one group of students. They create routines and patterns that give the day form and meaning.

"I live in my own little world in my classroom. Sometimes I think that my children and I share a secret life that is off limits to anyone else. We just go about our business, like so many peas in a pod."

For secondary teachers, the daily rhythm is more externally determined. Bells ring to signal the passing of classes, each of which will spend some parcel of time with the teacher in his or her classroom. Though students may move throughout the building, high school teachers often never leave their rooms in the course of a day. For every "period" or "hour," there is a routine: taking attendance, continuing from yesterday, introducing today's material, winding down, and making an assignment for tomorrow. Repeated five times a day, such routines become fixed and life becomes predictable.

In the course of a day, activities and interactions multiply, energy fluctuates. Elementary teachers may organize activities to accommodate the ebb and flow of the students' and their own energies. There are quiet times and active times, times set aside for individual attention, large-group instruction, small-group work, and seatwork. Secondary teachers may acknowledge that they are less effective during the first and last hours and more energetic during the middle of the day. The pace and depth of instruction are altered accordingly. For both elementary and secondary teachers, the school day is punctuated by interruptions: PA announcements, telephone calls and messages from the office, minor crises that need attending. All these become incorporated into the pattern of the day. Without missing a step, experienced teachers pick up where they left off.

Days merge into weeks. Monday is always difficult. So is Friday, but the difficulties are softened by the promise of the weekend. Midweek is optimal for teaching. The process—review, teach, test—fits neatly into the natural pace of weeks. Weeks become months and months become seasons. And each has its rhythms. Fall is the time of promise; new beginnings always bring hope. As the seasons progress, there is a downward spiral of energy until Thanksgiving, a perfectly timed and well-deserved break from the routine. There is a resurgence of sorts between Thanksgiving and Christmas, the most harried three weeks on any calendar. The Christmas break brings relief and buoys teachers and students for the final onslaught of the semester's end. January is brief. February is not; it is by far the longest month by any emotional measure.

"I always think of changing professions in February."

By March, the end is within sight and energies surge until the spring break, anticipated as much as the Christmas holiday and well appreciated. Then time passes quickly. There is the last-minute rush to get everything in and to meet the promises made in September by early June. The final weeks are filled with activities—final testing and grading, promotions, graduation, end-of-the-year events. And then, quite arbitrarily, on a Friday in June it all stops. Teachers and students go their separate ways. For ten weeks, there are no routines, no shared rituals, no school. The patterns that were learned and shared rudely come to an end, to be recreated in the fall when the cycle begins again. Such are the rhythms of teaching.

Rules

Like any profession, teaching has its rules—some codified and formal, others tacitly accepted and informal "rules of thumb." Two such rules may be simply stated: *Be practical. Be private.* Some further elaboration aids us in understanding the effect of these simple rules of behavior for teachers.

After years of formal academic preparation, most teachers enter teaching and experience a common jolt. Equipped with theoretical understandings, they lack the practical knowledge that they need for survival.

Education courses in and of themselves are quite theoretical. To be sure, they are helpful as far as background material goes, but there is no substitute for actual *practical* experience . . . My three year stint of duty as a housemaster and teacher . . . gave me a great deal of *practical* experience in learning more about young people and how to handle young people (Lortie, 1965).

Practical knowledge in schools is defined in terms of its opposites. Being practical is the opposite of being theoretical; being practical is the opposite of being idealistic. University professors are theoretical; inexperienced teachers are idealistic. New teachers in search of practical knowledge, then, must reject the university professors who trained them as well as their own tendencies to seek ideal solutions to difficult problems. Practical knowledge is lodged in the experiences and practices of teachers at work in their classrooms. It is to other teachers and to oneself that the novice must turn for practical ideas.

What makes an idea practical? First, it develops from the circumstance of the school. Second, it has immediate application. Third, it is offered by practical people. Finally, it addresses practical problems. Practical people are those who are or have recently been teachers. Practical school problems include discipline, attendance, order, and achievement. Practical ideas require little additional work or preparation; they fit into the existing rhythms of the school. Practical ideas are immediate and concrete and can be effected with the resources and structures that currently exist.

> *"No teacher ever does what he or she thinks is best. We do the best we can in the circumstances. What you think is a good idea from the outside turns out to be impossible in the classroom."*

To be practical means to concentrate on products and processes; to draw on experience rather than research; to be short-range and not predictive in thinking or planning.

As an opposite to idealism, practicality values adjustment, accommodation, and adaptation. Idealism is identified with youth; it does not wear well in the adult "real world" of teaching. New teachers are initiated into the practicality ethic during their first year on the job. They learn their "place" in the school organization, to keep quiet when private principles are violated by public practices, and to be politic about what they say and to whom they say it. To be practical, in this sense, is to accept the school as it is and to adapt. Striving to change the system is idealistic; striving to make do is practical. Concern for each student's well-being and optimal learning is idealistic; acceptance of limitations of student potential and teacher influence is practical. Reflective self-criticism is idealistic; expressing the belief "I do the best I can; it's just that the kids don't try" is practical. Being open to change and to outside influences is idealistic; being self-sufficient is practical. Being practical saves one from shame and doubt. It is a useful rule to follow.

The practicality rule has a corollary; that is, be private. In effect, it is practical to be private. What does being private mean? It means not sharing experiences about teaching, about classes, about students, about perceptions.

> *"I don't know what it's like in business or industry. It may be the same. I don't know how friendly co-workers are, how honest they are. It just seems*

*that in teaching, teachers really are unwilling to be honest with each other,
I think, to confide with each other about professional things and personal
things."*

By following the privacy rule, teachers forfeit the opportunity to display
their successes; but they also gain. They gain the security of not having
to face their failures publicly and losing face.

Being private also means staking out a territory and making it one's
own. For most teachers, that territory is the individual classroom.

Teachers have a sense of "territoriality" and an "ideology" [which] includes a
belief of the inviolability of a teacher's classroom (McPherson, 1972).

To ensure their claim, teachers seldom invite each other into their classes.
Observation is equated with evaluation, and evaluation violates one's
sense of place and position in the world.

In being private, each teacher makes an individual and conscious
choice to go it alone.

*"Me? You get to a point. I made a personal decision. I know a lot of teachers
have done the same thing. You seal off the room and you deal with the
students. You say, 'you and me and let's see what we can do alone.' "*

Most schools do not provide meaningful supervision, and most teachers
do not ask for it. The very act of teaching is invisible to one's peers.

*"It is safer to be private. There is some safety in the tradition, even though
it keeps you lonely."*

Loneliness and isolation are high prices to pay, but teachers willingly
pay them when the alternatives are seen as exposure and censure. When
asked in whom he confides about his days, one man replied with some
sense of irony and sadness, "My wife."

Interactions

Given the power of classroom territoriality, it comes as no surprise
that the most important and immediate interactions that teachers have
are with their students.

*"You work with kids. That's what you do. And a school is a place that will
allow you to do that."*

Since, as noted earlier, almost all rewards come from students, relationships with them are primary in the constellation of interactions in a school. For elementary teachers, the focus on children is a taken-for-granted phenomenon.

"I'm with my children all day long. I watch them change by the moment. Some days they'll tell me all of their secrets. Other days, they withdraw into their own little shells. Whatever they do, I'm there to see and hear it, and I take it all to heart."

For secondary teachers, relationships with students are more fragmented and are mediated through the subject matter.

"It is the subject matter and the kids. I love the subject matter and naturally you need an audience for that. The kids are the audience and they're important to me. I can't teach my subject matter without touching the kids in some way."

In either case, relationships with students are daily, direct, sometimes conflictual, but always central.

"I dream about them. I have nightmares about them. I can't lose them. It is worse on vacation. When I'm in school and it's late October and I've accepted that I'm really back, then the dreams finally stop."

For most, it is the personal interaction rather than instructional interaction that is most valued. This is true on the secondary level as well as on the elementary level.

"If someone told me that my job is just to teach math, I would quit. I couldn't stand to see myself as someone who teaches skills and nothing else. I have to feel that I am doing something more lasting."

What is that "something more lasting"? It has to do with influencing and guiding children toward adulthood, with serving as a moral presence, with having a stake in the future.

"When you realize that what you say in the classroom—even though you think no one is listening—has an effect on your students, you realize that you are a role model, even if you don't see yourself that way. The kids take what I have to say, think about it, and make decisions based on it. I have

that kind of influence . . . it's scary but it makes me feel good. It's a big responsibility."

Such involvement has its rewards both in the present and in the future.

"I like to see them when they come back, so I can see how they're doing, how they're turning out. I love to watch them grow. It's terrific. It's true with any age group—you can see the growth and development. Let's hope it continues. They're so cute. They are all individuals and they bubble about certain things. Some of them, my God, are so brave. . . ."

We cannot overstate the importance of teacher-student interactions. When the rewards from these interactions are plentiful, teachers are energized and thrive. When the rewards from these interactions are diminished, teachers lose that part of themselves that is most self-sustaining and most central to the well-being of the profession.

If teaching is to be understood as a "lonely profession," then the source of that loneliness lies outside of the realm of children. It is posited in the realm of interactions with other adults, especially one's peers. While relations with students tend to be immediate, direct, and engaging, relations with peers may be characterized as remote, oblique, and defensively protective. The rule of privacy governs peer interactions in a school. It is all right to talk about the news, the weather, sports, and sex. It is all right to complain in general about the school and the students. However, it is not acceptable to discuss instruction and what happens in classrooms as colleagues.

"If I were to go into the lounge and say, 'I've had a great class. The kids are really interesting. They were on the board, asking great questions, and they really got from me what I wanted them to,' no one would respond."

"I have never heard another teacher say, 'I have a problem.' You just don't do it. You solve the problem on your own, or you pretend that you don't have one. You never open up to anyone about anything important."

For most teachers in most schools, teaching is indeed a lonely enterprise. With so many people engaged in so common a mission in so compact a space and time, it is perhaps the greatest irony—and the greatest tragedy of teaching—that so much is carried on in self-imposed and professionally sanctioned isolation.

Our discussion of interactions is not complete until we consider the relation between teachers and principal in a building. Although face-to-face interactions with the principal may not be all that common, especially in a large urban high school, the relationship with one's principal is of paramount importance in a teacher's work life. A principal sets a tone.

"I think a principal can make or break a school in terms of—not even the day-to-day functioning—but in terms of the umbrella of attitudes and emotions."

That umbrella covers a wide area. The principal has the power to make working in a school pleasant or unbearable; that is quite a bit of power. A principal who makes teaching pleasant is one who trusts the staff to perform classroom duties with competence, and who deals with parents and the community in a way that supports teachers' decisions and safeguards against personal attacks.

Teachers avoid "getting on the bad side" of a principal; such a position makes life unbearable. The principal has the power to make extra duty assignments, to criticize classroom practices, to assign undesirable class schedules. More importantly, on an informal level, being disliked by the principal carries with it distinct psychological disadvantages.

"If I see him in the hall and he doesn't smile or look at me, I'm upset all day. What did I do wrong? Why doesn't he like me? Will he listen to me if there's a problem? I know it shouldn't affect me, but it does."

When teachers view a principal as critical or punishing, they are less likely to take risks and try new approaches. When teachers view a principal as supporting and rewarding, they are more able to approach the principal for support in trying something new, in securing resources, in gaining permission for special undertakings.

The relationship of teacher to principal is one of gaining access to privilege, and almost all privileges are arbitrarily in the hands of the principal. This is especially true for teachers who themselves aspire to administrative positions. The principal's recommendation about the administrative potential of teachers is taken seriously. While many teachers profess that they avoid the principal and learn to work around him or her, the importance of that office is always felt in the daily life of the school.

Feelings

Strong feelings accompany intense and varied interactions. The feelings of teachers about their work and their lives are complex, characterized by conflict, frustration, satisfaction, and joy.

When we characterized teacher-student interactions as the major source of rewards for teachers, we placed great emphasis on feelings of genuine satisfaction that accrue from these relationships. The other side of those feelings, of living one's professional life always in the company of children, is also quite powerful for teachers. These other feelings are more negative and often come to light in the company of other adults who work in "the real world," not the world of schools.

> "I had a disagreement with my mother-in-law the other day. I don't remember what it was about—taxes or something that is being voted on. Every time I started to talk, she would disagree and then tell me that I didn't live in the real world, that I spent all of my time with kids, and that I just didn't know about business and other things. I felt very angry. That kind of thing happens now and again. I feel that I do live in the real world, but people who don't teach don't think that's true."

To the rest of the world, teachers often seem to be living in a child's reality and are viewed as not being able to function as adults in an adult world. This perception leaves teachers uneasy at best, defensive at worse, almost always self-doubting, and characteristically ambivalent about their roles and their constant relationship with young people.

Feelings of self-doubt are exacerbated by the absence of a standard by which one can measure one's professional competence. The lack of peer support and interaction makes it difficult to develop a clear sense of the quality of one's own teaching. Teaching skills are evaluated by the students, whose judgment is not always trustworthy, and by oneself.

> "It took me ten years to feel that I was a good teacher. In fact, I would try very hard not to miss a day of school. I thought if a substitute came in and taught my classes that all the students would find out how bad I was and how good someone else was."

There is a general lack of confidence, a pervasive feeling of vulnerability, a fear of being "found out." Such feelings are made worse because of the privacy ethic. There is no safe place to air one's uncertainties and to get the kind of feedback necessary to reduce the anxiety about being a good teacher, or at least an adequate one.

One way a teacher may gain some confidence is to define a sphere of control. For most, that is the classroom. It becomes essential to gain and maintain dominance if one is to survive.

"When I'm in my classroom, I know I'm in control. I can teach the way I want to teach, do what I want to do."

Once inside the classroom, a teacher knows that all control is tenuous. It depends on a negotiated agreement between students and the teacher. If that agreement is violated, a teacher will subordinate all teaching activities to one primary goal: to regain and maintain control. Keeping a class in order is the only visible indication to one's colleagues and principal that one is, in fact, a good teacher. When one loses control, one loses everything.

Feelings about control are made more problematic by the awareness on the part of teachers that once outside the classroom, their control is severely limited. Within the formal organization of the school, teachers have little authority in making decisions that affect their environment. Teachers, then, move from a level of almost complete authority to a level of powerlessness. This being in-and-out-of-control leads to feelings of frustration and resignation to the ways things are and will always be.

The feelings that surround issues of always being with children, of professional competence, and of being in-and-out-of-control are highly charged and little acknowledged. They should not be underestimated; these feelings often block a teacher's impulse to work to improve one's teaching or to influence what happens in the school.

Rhythms, Rules, Interactions, and Feelings

In this section, we have tried to present a view of some of the day-to-day realities of schools for the teachers who work there. We have concentrated on rhythms, rules, interactions, and feelings as a way to gain some insight into schools and how to make them better. We may summarize by saying:

● By understanding rhythms, we come to realize that years are cyclical; that time in schools is finite; that patterns often supplant purpose; that what has been done may be undone in the seasons that follow; and that what has not yet been done is still in the realm of the possible.

- By understanding rules, we come to accept the limits of rational plans, the inevitability of resistance, the power of collective sanctions, and the inviolability of individuals and their classrooms.
- By understanding interactions, we come to an awareness of the centrality of children in teachers' lives, of the unrealized potential of colleagueship, and of the power of a principal to make a school better or worse.
- By understanding feelings, we appreciate ambiguity, vulnerability, and defensiveness as camouflages for commitment, concern, and hope; and we come to value patience and realism as guideposts for our own actions.

References

Bentzen, Mary. *Changing the Magic Feather Principle.* New York: McGraw-Hill, 1975.

Doyle, Walter, and Ponder, Gerald A. "The Practicality Ethic in Teacher Decision Making." *Interchange* 8, 3 (1977–78).

Emrick, John, and Peterson, Susan. *A Synthesis of Findings: Five Recent Studies of Educational Dissemination and Change.* San Francisco: Far West Laboratories, 1978.

Geoffrey, William. *Complexities of an Urban Classroom.* New York: Holt, Rinehart & Winston, 1968.

Goodlad, John I. *The Dynamics of Educational Change.* New York: McGraw-Hill, 1975.

Gross, Neal; Giacquinta, Joseph B.; and Bernstein, Marilyn. *Implementing Organizational Innovations.* New York: Basic Books, 1971.

Jackson, Philip. *Life in Classrooms.* New York: Holt, Rinehart & Winston, 1968.

Lortie, Dan C. "Teacher Socialization: The Robinson Crusoe Model." In *The Real World of the Classroom Teacher,* Report of the 1965 National TEPS Conference. Washington, D.C.: National Education Association, 1965.

McPherson, Gertrude. *Small Town Teacher.* Cambridge: Harvard University Press, 1972.

Sarason, S.B.; Levine, M.; Goldenberg, I.; Cherlin, D.; and Bennett, E. *Psychology in Community Settings.* New York: John Wiley & Sons, 1966.

Shiman, David A., and Lieberman, Ann. "Non-Model for Schools." *Educational Forum* 38, 4 (May 1974).

Smith, Louis, and Keith, Pat. *Anatomy of an Educational Innovation.* New York: Wiley, 1971.

Sussman, Leila. *Tales Out of School: Implementing Organizational Change in the Elementary Grades.* Philadelphia: Temple University Press, 1977.

Waller, Willard. *The Sociology of Teaching.* New York: John Wiley, 1967.

2

Teaching and Learning in the Elementary School: A Three-Ring Circus

Review and reconstruction of the process for the sake of learning is our best hope, and that is extraordinarily difficult for anyone, let alone people of action.

—Seymour Sarason, 1972

In this chapter, we explore the social realities of teaching more concretely. We begin where public schooling begins: in the elementary school. Our research has taken us to many classrooms, but one in particular stands out. It is here that we choose to focus our attention.

The classroom is part of a magnet program, housed within a traditional elementary school. The two teachers who team-teach here are veterans; each has been in the business for almost 30 years. What makes this classroom and our research in it most unique is that we share a common history with the teacher we study. Having known each other since college, Ann Lieberman and the two teachers entered into a very special and strong relationship between researcher and researched. Lieberman did more than observe, take copious notes, and raise carefully worded questions. She participated in the life of the classroom, becoming a "third hand" in the instructional program. Conversely, the teachers did more than serve as the objects of study. They became active subjects, formulating their own questions, testing their own hypotheses, and building their own theories. What resulted was a mosaic of activity and reflection about elementary teaching, a mosaic that informs a major portion of our thinking about the realities of elementary teaching.

The First Two Days: Activity and Reflections

We concentrate here on the first two days of a new school year. By attending to the details of these days, we build understandings about teaching and learning in an elementary school.

Day One

The school year starts off with a half-day session during which the teachers begin to test students to find out where they are and what they know in reading and math. An introductory social studies lesson on the United States includes a discussion of the Presidential election (high interest), the Constitution, and how the two are related. Students are given a handout with a few questions and the Preamble to the Constitution. There is also a handwriting lesson for which students are to write something about themselves. This lesson forms the basis for a bulletin board display that appears the next day. The title on the bulletin board is "ABOUT ME." Under the title are 3 × 5 cards that read:
"I ran in the 50-yard dash and won. John."
"I suck my thumb, I'm skinny, and I love school! Jeffrey."
"My brother left for college. Tracy."
"I have one sister who's younger than I am; my father died of a heart attack. My mother is a teacher. I must come to class. Evie."

Day Two

8:30—The buses are lining up outside. Six children come in; one races up to the teacher and announces that he has already learned the Preamble. Mrs. T. hugs the student. "How did you do that in one night?" The student replies, "I did it during the commercials of *Shogun*. There were a lot of them." The teacher glances to the floor where several girls are gathered. "What slob lives here?" (This directed to a huge mess of lunch, books, and papers on the floor.) Nicole replies, "It's mine. I'll put it all away." Another student, Stacey, hobbles in, barely able to walk. It is clear that her feet are killing her; she's wearing the latest style high wedge shoes. Mrs. T. efficiently heads to the closet to retrieve a pair of canvas flat shoes for Stacey to wear. "Don't ever wear those shoes to school again." The student nods in agreement, indicating her relief.

As students come off the bus, they look on the board, and within ten minutes they're working on individual tasks. The choices of assignments grow as the week goes on. Both teachers have announced and are already reinforcing their organizational structure in relation to the children. They have put times on the board for particular activities and names under the times; for instance:

Reading 10:40	*Spelling 11:35*
Stacy, Mark	Amoko, John, Sue
Joann, Ellen, Ariel	Barbara
Steve, Pat	

Other assignments are listed with names of students who have not completed their work. In this way students know what is expected of them, and the teachers have a way of keeping track of the various activities.

By 9:10 all 60 students are present and ready to begin a class meeting. They sit on couches, floor, and chairs. Both teachers tell the students, "This is not a time to talk with neighbors. Sharon and Sue know how to come to a class meeting." Mrs. B. explains, "If assignments are not finished, take your work home for homework. Every day there will be a writing assignment. It will say 'writing' on the board. Every day there will be a reading assignment. Every week you will be required to do at least three learning center assignments that are set up around the room. There are ten to choose from." As the students begin to get restless, the teachers quickly shift to a social studies lesson on the Constitution, which is followed by a brief question and answer period. Mrs. B. then asks the students what the first ten amendments to the Constitution are called. No one knows. After ten minutes of wrestling with some very abstract concepts that the students struggle to understand, the room fills with a deadly silence. In a low and very mysterious voice, Mrs. T. says to the class, "Don't anybody tell if they know, but tomorrow come prepared to tell us what the first ten amendments are called and why they are so called." The students giggle with delight and anticipation.

The two teachers share recess duty, each getting ten minutes off and ten minutes supervising on the playground.

When students return from recess they have ten minutes of silent reading while the teachers quickly prepare for the next activity, a diagnostic math test that serves as an initial basis for grouping students. Those who finish early go to a center to work while others complete their test.

And so the day goes with movement back and forth from small groups to individualized activities to large-group instruction, with the teachers weaving back and forth, giving immediate feedback, correcting papers, encouraging, and reprimanding when things get out of hand. In just two days, the teachers have introduced their students to the rules, rhythms, and routines of the classroom. They have established norms about behavior and expectations about achievement. They have begun the process of educating and socializing children. Beneath the constant flux of activity and the intensity of interaction, we can begin to see another dimension of teaching: the tensions and conflicts of the job, what Dan Lortie calls the "endemic uncertainties" of teaching.

Endemic uncertainties complicate the teaching craft and hamper the earning of psychic rewards. Intangibility and complexity impose a toll . . . it is most unlikely that so many teachers would experience difficulty if effective solutions were at hand (Lortie, 1975, p. 159).

What are these dilemmas? What causes these inherent tensions? In the next section, we explore the answers to these questions as we examine three major dilemmas or tensions as they begin to emerge from our description of the "first two days."

Personal and Professional Dilemma

In the greatest sense, being a teacher of a group presents teachers with an overarching dilemma—that of the tension between the personal and the professional (Sarason, 1971). The teachers we observed display a superb feel for moving back and forth between familiarity, liking, caring, warmth, and a more detached teacher-like stance where one describes the procedures of a learning center.

"Everyone can make a choice of three centers. Be sure to finish your work. I'm waiting! (Lights dim.) Most of you understand that signal. Ernie and Tracey, that is wonderful work. . . ."

One gathers as much information as possible about the children in a classroom, but it is hard to do justice to every child in the group. And the huge amount of subject matter that is taught in elementary classrooms makes it virtually impossible to be expert in everything. This is where a teacher's own sense of creativity takes over. Given many children and much subject matter, routine becomes easier than risk. And dropping a subject or two is better than the insecurity of teaching something you know little about.

The established teacher has been playing it safe so long that she has lost the necessary minimum of recklessness without which life becomes painful (Waller, 1967).

Domination and Control Dilemma

It is too simple to tally the amount of teacher or student talk or to make light of the tremendous role of discipline, control, or what turns out to be a replay of the personal and professional dilemma. The key problem for the elementary teacher is to establish routines that offer some semblance of stability to the maze of students, curriculum, time, and materials at hand. To do this the teacher must have control over the class. By quickly establishing those routines, our two teachers created an order in the class that would endure throughout the school year.

The folklore among teachers of intimidating the children *first* and then becoming friendly stems from a need to quickly establish routines that allow the teacher and students to move ahead with the work (Smith and Geoffrey, 1968). At its worst, this means that teachers establish rigid routines where the clock, the book, and the test are used to control students. At its best, this approach means that teachers control direct instructional activities such as reading, writing, and math, and have more flexibility in many other subjects.

A certain conflict of interest must always exist between the person who rules and the one who is ruled (Waller, 1967).

Universal Tensions

All elementary teachers face "universal tensions." The way they respond to these tensions often defines what kind of teachers they become. Among the most common of these tensions are the following:

1. How can we teach all these subjects in some defensible manner in the amount of time allotted in the school day? These teachers had

from 8:30 to 2:20, when the buses arrived to take students to different parts of the city.

2. How does one keep interest alive in light of many competing stimuli? These teachers did well. The Preamble existed side by side with *Shogun*; it was clear they were sensitive to the outside world and the specific problems of building a community at school.

3. How can children be grouped to allow for differences among them and still keep the community together? The learning abilities these teachers had to address ranged from the 2nd grade to the 11th grade level.

4. The more varied the set of activities in the classroom, the more the teacher has to attend to record keeping, feedback, novelty, and the greater risk of losing control. Again, the teachers here were outstanding in the amount of variety they presented to students in order to engage their interest. But these teachers have had over ten years of experience in team teaching, and they have learned together. Most teachers do not have this opportunity. These teachers have created their own learning community with each other.

5. The pressure to teach the three Rs and at the same time cover material forces the teacher into moving back and forth between coverage and mastery (Kepler, 1980). These teachers decided that the students had to learn the three Rs and they monitored closely. Other activities were handled more flexibly. But regardless of the teacher, little or no help is forthcoming to aid in these decisions. And most improvement efforts impinge heavily on these tensions, already a large part of the teacher's work day.

6. Given the dailiness of teaching and the age of elementary students, teachers are forced to say things in a very simple fashion. The problem then becomes how to maintain one's integrity as an adult, while always translating into elementary language. Being with young children all day every day has its effects on the teacher.

In a way, the teacher gets shut out of both worlds. She is clearly not a member of the child's culture, but who else spends their time currying favor with young children as a major source of rewards? (Peltzman, 1975).

Teacher, 33 years old:
"I knew something was wrong when I began to skip out of school."

Kindergarten teacher:
"I told my 40-year-old brother to be sure and put on his galoshes. Wow! Did he give me a strange look!"

7. The very act of being with children, translating complex ideas into child-like terms, struggling to make the world comprehensible to young children, is both exciting and stressful. What one does with children and their success in translating the world is what makes teachers feel that they are doing a good job. But the greater the internal classroom community and esprit, the greater the distance from one's peers and the more impervious one gets to ideas from the outside.

"We don't talk to anyone! We have a huge following. We have parents who bring all their brothers and sisters to our class."

8. Much of the learning about how to manage one's classroom gets set early in one's teaching career. Awareness, reflection, and the possibilities for improvement are rarely provided in schools.

It is not possible to develop the personalities of students favorably without giving like opportunities to teachers, and it is not possible to liberate students without liberating teachers (Waller, 1967, p. 445).

9. Many urban schools now have multi-ethnic groups and children with special needs in their classrooms. Many teachers have not been prepared in any way to deal with these differences.

10. In most elementary classrooms, teachers must pick up where the last teacher left off. That often causes an additional source of tension in the teacher's world.

"Kids come well prepared from B.J.'s room, but not from Room 12."

Here again, we see each teacher inheriting the riches or the rags from the previous teacher with little or no dialogue among colleagues about expectations.

In summary, what we see as standard fare in elementary schools are teachers who are responsible for ten or more subject areas. Somehow the subjects need to be organized and managed with a group of 23 to 26 children. Teachers wrestle with how to group students for different activities; they must decide what to teach and what to drop; and they must decide how much time to spend on one area versus another. Pressure for the mastery of the three Rs limits the amount of time spent on other parts of the curriculum.

The common sense understandings which teachers have of their problems bites deeper into reality than do the meanderings of most theorists. Teachers will do well to insist that any program of educational reform shall start with them, that it shall be based upon, and shall include their common sense insight (Waller, 1967).

Implications for School Improvement

Now we come to the crux of the problem. Teachers have learned how to teach by teaching. They have learned techniques, sensitivities, and insights from many trials and many more errors. Most have learned what they know in isolation from peers; as a result, they cling tightly to what has been forged in struggle. How then do we come to deal with and understand that there are many teaching styles learned along the way, and many strengths and weaknesses gained. Being defensive is probably more common than being open; complaining about the previous year's teacher is more common than complaining about oneself; surviving the onslaught of this year's mandate is probably more prevalent than being excited about a new skill; complaining in the teacher's room about a difficult group takes priority over collective group struggle with ideas about teaching. These are all legitimate problems. They will always be part of the teacher culture as long as the major part of teaching is learned experientially. But they give us a clue as to how to intervene and make possible ways to open up to new experience.

We suggest that there are four major components for dealing with the reality of teachers' styles and modes of learning. These components were touched on in Chapter 1 and are examined more closely here. They present an honest description of the social context of the school, the teachers, the substance to be used for improvement, and the interpersonal relations among the school personnel. We discuss them separately even though we know that they are in constant interaction with each other. We then present two case studies in which these components were used to move from abstraction to reality.

The Social Context

Schools exist within a social context. That context may be as broad as the national climate for education or as narrow as the conditions of the local neighborhood surrounding the school.

On the national level, we are currently engaged in a great debate about the quality of public schooling. That debate has tended to accept merit pay, career ladders, and more stringent requirements for teaching as among the best strategies for improving schools. All these strategies take as givens that most teachers are not meritorious and that most people who enter teaching are less than adequate. Such a national consensus contributes to low teacher morale. The national debate has filtered down to the local level where concern about staff evaluation, salary, and termination affect the daily work of teachers. In addition, on the local level, immediate conditions such as school closings, student enrollment decline, and reduction-in-force take their toll. Add to that specific concerns about student discipline and achievement and one gets a sense of the enormity of the effect of the local context on schools and teachers.

When we consider social context, then, we look at both societal issues and local concerns; they may be intimately related or one level of concern may dominate.[1] Nonetheless, social context is a critical component of school improvement. An understanding of the environmental pressures on the school provides us with an appreciation of what teachers are feeling, how they see their work, and what they are ready for. Some questions specifically aimed at elementary school might be:

- Where is the school in terms of current national problems in elementary schools? (Is the mood avoidance? discussion? gossip?)
- What are the central pressures on the particular school?
- How is the school organized? (By teams, grade levels, informal groups, every one for him/herself?)
- Are there any "idea champions" in the school?[2]
- What are the givens? (School closings, weak principal, aging faculty, new superintendent?)

The Teachers

Who are the teachers? What are they like? How long have they been there? What are their experiences with children, with innovative ideas, with teaching, with groups? If local conditions are dominant in school improvement efforts, how do those conditions relate to the teachers?

We have noted that teachers learn to teach by experiencing trial and error in their own classrooms. Furthermore, isolation from other adults, for the most part, is the predominant social milieu of teachers (Sarason

---

[1] For examples of works that emphasize the local context of change, see Gross, Giacquinta, and Bernstein (1971); McPherson (1972); Sarason (1971); Smith and Keith (1971); and Sussman (1977).

[2] Idea champions are people internal to the school who are enthusiastic about a particular idea and are willing to speak out for it (Daft and Becker, 1978).

and others, 1966). Both of these conditions create an understandable tension that teachers feel about improving their craft. On the one hand, "No one knows my class the way I do," but I also know that "even when I'm good, I'm never good enough." Morale is so low in so many schools that to pretend it isn't is to deceive oneself. Some questions that might guide us are:

- Where are the teachers in this school in terms of sharing with each other? (Do teachers in this elementary school eat together, share children, ever talk to one another?)
- Is there a problem, concern, subject area, idea that is of general concern—general enough to engage the 1st grade as well as the 6th grade teacher? (Do teachers complain about collective problems? Do they have any means to share what might be collective concerns?)
- Is there a teacher, librarian, someone within the school who is sensitive to teachers, who trusts them and is trusted?

The Substance

Ideas, projects, packages, materials, processes, mandates, problems, new subject areas, research translations are all grist for improvement efforts. The key here is that different schools, depending on their social contexts and the talents and abilities of individuals, deal differently with substance. In a school where there has been tremendous disruption of both teachers and pupils, a major issue might be getting people to talk with one another. In this instance, initiating processes that allow for better communication is the substance. On the other hand, in a school or district having a relatively stable population, where people have grown too comfortable in the face of growing problems, using research that has been translated into practical activities may be an effective means to get people involved. In this situation, some of the recent research on teacher effectiveness might be the substance of discussion for the faculty (Denham and Lieberman, 1980; Brookover and Lezotte, 1979). Many schools suffer a general malaise affecting both faculty and students. In this kind of school, finding a way to get people to talk about a major problem area could be the substance of a development effort. The major task is to get people involved in *their* definition of the problem, *their* view of a meaningful activity. These discussions must eventually have action proposals, or people will quickly lose interest and go back to their splendid isolation.

Again, the substance of any improvement effort can come from a variety of different sources. The problem has been, for some, a barrage of substance, yanking and pulling teachers in a variety of ways, making assumptions that teaching is a series of interchangeable techniques. For others it has been the "mandate by memo"—an unrealistic, simplistic view of how classrooms are organized, the complexity of the teacher's work, and the herculean efforts needed to really make changes. Well-developed ideas need time to be adapted to classroom life (McLaughlin and Marsh, 1979; Cooper and Leiter, 1978). And underdeveloped ideas need discussion, activities, trial and error, and time to work on them through experiential means (Sussman, 1977). But both need supportive conditions, often *in class* personalized help, participation from peers, moral support from the principal. Changing a routine that has been learned over the years is incredibly complicated. And it is made all the more so in schools because of the solo nature of most teaching. Substance that penetrates teaching style will be meaningless unless it involves teachers in ways that relate to *their* understandings, *their* types of students, neighborhood, grade level—all matched with a sensitivity to *their* classroom reality. Some questions we might pose are:

• What ideas are being pressed on the elementary schools? (A diagnostic reading program, mainstreaming, new population or program, latest research?)
• How can these ideas be made practical?
• What provisions are there for teachers to talk and discuss the idea?
• How can talk be moved to action in the school?
• What first steps can be taken by teachers to try out some new possibilities and discuss them with colleagues?

Interpersonal Relations Among School Personnel

Perhaps the most ignored area of observations about schools is the one most obvious to teachers—the interpersonal relations in the building. These relations are difficult to capture because they are so ubiquitous, but they may be the most important determinants to teachers' feelings about self, about work, about peers, and most definitely about the principal.

"My principal was wonderful. He used to tell me to stay home when I got fed up with the kids. 'Take some time for yourself. It will be worth it. You will feel replenished.' So I did. I would take a day off, go shopping. But I found myself sneaking around the racks of clothes wondering whether

anyone would know that I was playing hooky and wondering whether the sub was destroying all that I had built with the kids."

The relationship between teacher and principal may be a more dominant feature in school life than the larger social issues in the newspapers and the recent research done on the processes of school change (Meyer, 1975; Deal and Celotti, 1977; Brazill, 1979; Hall and others, 1980). The principal (especially in the elementary school) makes it known what is important, what will not be tolerated, and, in a strange way, sets the tone for tension, warmth, openness, fear. We have worked in schools where a beehive of teacher activity was literally destroyed by an insecure principal (Miller and Wolf, 1979); or the opposite, a school come alive through the valiant efforts of a principal sensitive to teachers' modes of work and their insecurities (Chesler, 1975).

In a large-scale study, teachers were found to be very affected in both their work life and their feelings about themselves by the behavior and activities of the principal (Lieberman, 1969). The difficulty is that teachers as a group become a personality in interaction with the principal and affect each other in different ways, which are not always consistent. But there is no doubt that the morale and the teachers' sense of professionalism has a great deal to do with the principal's treatment of the faculty. It is through the principal that all kinds of messages get relayed to teachers, and they can come with caring and sensitivity, as orders from headquarters, or with distance and coldness.

As couples may be loosely tied to each other, so are teachers with their principal—more so in elementary than in secondary schools. The relationship is, first of all, very tenuous. It hangs together by various exchanges of conversation, and assignments of rooms, students, or materials. There are offhand comments like "This room ought to be cleaner." "Don't forget about the fire drill Friday." "Mrs. S. came to visit me yesterday. She says Karen is not happy." (No further comment or details). Teachers may perceive the principal's body language as being supportive or disparaging. Or they may pick up the impression that the principal is more concerned with order and tidiness or the latest district mandate than with people.

But then each partner of the couple has other vital relationships. For the teacher, the students are far more important than anyone. For the principal, parents, maybe other principals, and definitely the district office are ties that create both pressure and satisfaction. So the members of the couple inhabit the same building, need each other, yet carry on many other relationships that are salient to them.

Perhaps, even more difficult is the fact that each member of the couple doesn't really have a good understanding of what the other one does.

Teachers about principal:
"He is always shuffling papers and walking around."
"He doesn't have the slightest idea of what J and I are doing."
"I can't imagine a football blocker who is better than Ms. W. at getting in the way of movement."

Principal about teachers:
"I know she comes on strong, and I don't know what to do about it."
"She's been screaming at the kids for years, but they know what to expect from her."
"I felt I was a referee at a boxing match. First the parent gave her complaints, then the teacher gave hers. They were both right, but both coming from different places."

Teachers all claim that once people leave the classroom, they lose the dailiness and closed-in feeling of teaching as well as their sensitivity to classroom realities. So, too, with many principals whose own demands on their time often distance them from teachers.

Yet, they need each other. The principal can set a tone, fight for teachers, relate to them sensitively and provide for an environment that makes a difference in teachers' feelings about self, work, and school improvement (Lieberman, 1969; Berman and McLaughlin, 1974,) or make an offhand comment that feels like a blow on the head:

"I have been working day and night to prepare for a 4–5 combination grade. I have previously taught 3rd grade. And, to make matters worse, I had to change my room. I finally felt good about the beginning of the semester and my new class. The principal came by and said, 'What are those boxes doing here?' Can you imagine how I felt?"
"I run this school like a concentration camp—only more flexibly."

Teachers and Other Teachers

It is hard for outsiders to understand why it is so difficult to share with one's colleagues in an elementary school. It has been noted that the teaching enterprise suffers from a lack of technical language (Lortie, 1975), and that teachers form their repertoire by immediacy and pragmatic responses to daily demands (Jackson, 1968). It is true that anecdotes form a common mode of expression among teachers, thereby making it difficult to communicate big ideas about what one is doing. But it is more than that. Even when teachers are spectacular by anyone's criteria, they are hard pressed to describe the complexity of what is going on.

The most successful teacher at Hartwick totally boycotts the education industry, is not unusually well read, would never intrude on another teacher's class and could not explain why he is successful. The prevailing wisdom at Hartwick is that either you have it or you don't when it comes to teaching students (Gibbon, 1979).

The tendency is to describe activities, events, interactions, incidents, hearsay, and gossip. This is easy to talk about in the few minutes that teachers have with each other over lunch, recess, or around the mimeograph machine.

> *"You've got to come see this giraffe. It just has a head and each time the kids read a book and report on it in some form they put up a piece of the tail. They are going crazy and they love it."*
>
> *"This mimeo is fantastic for vocabulary building. I will be through with it today. Do you want to use it?"*
>
> *"Let's do our Mayan calendars together. I can lead the art stuff and you can give the background. O.K.?"*

Improvement efforts are generally not described in activities or events, but come full blown with large conceptions like mastery learning, diagnostic/prescriptive teaching, mainstreaming, systematic instructional management strategies, Every Child a Winner.[3]

In some schools teachers come to work together and form close friendships outside of work. In others, teachers relate to each other only formally or on committees where they may go to meetings together. Or neither of these kinds of interactions may be evident. But it is clear that the atmosphere and what is encouraged or discouraged among teachers are intimately tied to the behaviors of the principal. We witness once

---

[3]These titles are described in *Educational Programs That Work*, Far West Laboratories, 1980.

again the delicate, yet sturdy, nature of elementary schools, tied together by loose, common characteristics: teachers in their own rooms with their students; principals who may be very involved with teachers or protective of their office or a variety of other modes; teachers interacting with each other in their own ways, a shorthand honed by the pragmatic and practical nature of their work. So any improvement effort involves the interpersonal relationships in the school, the predominance of the role of the principal, and the nature of the relationships among the teachers. Some questions we asked are:

• What is the state of the relationship between teachers and other teachers, and teachers and the principal?

• Do teachers relate easily and comfortably with the principal?

• Do teachers trust the principal?

• Do teachers trust each other?

• Is there a small group who is motivated to work with the principal's support?

• Is the dialogue that goes on in school realistically related to the conditions of the particular school and its most pressing problems as seen by principal and teachers?

• Are the people who make decisions about school improvement efforts aware that mobilizing teachers and engaging them in their own improvement is *the* reality (as differentiated from telling teachers what to do and assuming they will do it without their active involvement)?

• Is there an accurate assessment of what initially needs to be done to bring teachers together?

We have pulled apart the dynamics of what local school improvement in the elementary school involves. In reality, all of these parts are in dynamic interaction, and incidents, crises, good feelings, and dailiness are, for the most part, hidden from the outsider. We look at a few sample schools that show our components in action.

Case Studies

Larchmont School*

Larchmont school is in a large city. Until four years ago, the student population was predominately from upper-middle-class, white, profes-

---

*School names have been changed to protect confidentiality.

sional families. The school was considered a prize for any teacher who taught there. This year there has been court-ordered integration, massive busing, white flight, teacher transfers, and general disruption. The principal is well respected by parents and teachers alike. She respects the integration efforts even though she feels they have been mismanaged by people in higher administration. She knows the parents of the old population and is attempting to get to know the new. The teacher morale is low due to tremendous disruption in the school. Many active parents have transferred their children to private schools. The local school context appears to be chaotic.

The school has a long history of innovativeness, and a core of teachers is still involved in consistently improving their teaching, although some are uncomfortable with the bused children. The principal is clearly sensitive to the problem of working with teachers and to the chaos that the beginning of the year has brought. The principal is fully capable of leading an improvement effort that will deal with both the stability of the school and the attitude of teachers toward the old and the new children.

In this case, the most pressing problem will be to help school members by alleviating staff disruptions, room changes, and the insecurity of children transferring in and out of the school. The principal intends to begin a series of chats with the parents and to mobilize the teachers to work on their definition of the greatest problems they are having.

This principal and staff have easy and generally open, trustful relations with one another due to a history of supportive interpersonal relations. The teachers feel very committed to doing the best they can in spite of a general malaise that they describe as the worst beginning of the school year in the history of the district.

Larchmont school exemplifies, perhaps in the extreme, the dominance of the social context on a local school and how it must be considered, not as an aside, but often as the most critical component in a school improvement effort. The substance here will come from the teachers. While the principal builds a relationship with the parents, she will be holding meetings with the teachers to begin an examination of how best to deal with the new population.

Mayberry School District

This school district is small, suburban, and close-knit—a desirable place to live as well as to teach. There has been a history of great teacher autonomy and a general view that the schools are good. Currently the district is losing students as the families are getting older and younger families are not moving in. Like many suburban districts caught in an inflationary spiral, school closings and reductions in force have become major issues. The district is also typical of many in that there is growing pressure from parents for students to achieve, especially in the three Rs. All of the teachers in this district have been there at least six years, and most more than ten. But many of them are worried, fearing their jobs are on the line.

In general, the teachers are quite sophisticated, and most have Master's degrees. Many people, including the teachers, feel that extreme autonomy has kept teachers isolated from one another. Pressures to do better and to raise test scores have created a certain amount of disequilibrium in the schools and among administrators. The three principals of the schools do not generally share their problems with each other. The school board is supportive of the schools and is concerned with greater. accountability.

In this instance, the administration is using research reports on effective teaching as a source for school improvement. Figuring that the teachers would respect research if it could be made relevant to them and could be translated into usable ideas, district administrators have held meetings to discuss the research and its possible applications in classrooms. Although an outside person was hired to provide the initial stimulus, teachers quickly got involved.

As part of the inservice activities, teachers reported to each other successful lessons they had had and tried to describe what made them work. Discussion was spirited and teachers were highly engaged. But when asked if anyone would share their success story aloud, *no one volunteered.*

Concepts described in effective teaching research (feedback, monitoring, continuity) were used by teachers describing their own successful practices. Demonstration lessons were given and critiqued publicly by teachers *for the first time in the district.* Teachers participated in small-group discussions on three teaching dilemmas: (1) How do I deal with the mastery vs. coverage dilemma? (2) How do I know when students are successful? (3) How can I work to aid students in being independent learners?

These discussions revealed much of what we have described as the social realities of teaching—that trial and error and experience over time dominate the way teachers deal with dilemmas. But they also revealed a multitude of ways that teachers teach as they struggle with these dilemmas. The powerful effects of relating research to the realities of classroom life became evident.

These two cases represent two examples of tremendous differences in social context. In the first, the larger city context intruded on the local school to make city problems school problems. In the other, the predominant climate was stable, in spite of RIFs and school closings, and characterized mainly by teacher autonomy. The teachers manifested very different concerns in their different contexts. In the urban school immediate problems were dominant: how to understand and service culturally heterogeneous children in an unstable climate. In the other district the problem was breaking the business-as-usual climate and forcing an awareness of new conditions.

In the urban system, court-ordered busing made a focus for discussion obvious. In the other district, the extreme autonomy of the teachers made them insensitive to a changing social context. The substance for one group was how to work with a new population and how to create some semblance of stability amidst chaos. For the other group the substance was designed to confront teachers and create disequilibrium where there was complacency and stability.

We begin to see our four categories as means to assess the possibilities of school improvement at the local level; that is, in light of (1) the social context, (2) teacher characteristics, (3) the appropriate substance, and (4) the state of interpersonal relationships. The maze of mandates, meetings, memos, pressures, questions, and sensitivities to the ordinary routines that bind people together becomes the bedrock of school improvement activities.

Without attending to what is actually going on in a school, efforts at school improvement are a sham. Recognizing the elementary school with its "family orientation" forces us to call attention to the behavior and activities of people as they actually are. Then we must make distinctions, not among age, sex, or experience of the personnel, but how people relate to one another, how sensitive they are to one another, and how they learn to turn individual concerns into collective struggles.

References

Bentzen, Mary M. *Changing Schools: The Magic Feather Principle.* New York: McGraw-Hill, 1974.

Berman, Paul, and McLaughlin, Milbrey. *A Model of Educational Change: Federal Programs Supporting Educational Change, Volume I.* Santa Monica: Rand Corporation, 1974.

Brazill, Delores. "The Development and Implementation of a Comprehensive Elementary School Practices Survey in a New York City School District." Doctoral dissertation, Teachers College, Columbia University, 1979.

Brookover, W., and Lezotte, L. "Changes in School Characteristics Coincident with Changes in Student Achievement." Occasional Paper #17. East Lansing: Institute for Research on Teaching, Michigan State University, 1979.

Chesler, Mark, and others. *Desegregation-Integration: Planning for School Change.* Washington, D.C.: National Education Association, 1975.

Cooper, Myrna, and Leiter, M. "How Teacher Unionists View In-Service Education." *Teachers College Record* 80 (September 1978).

Denham, C., and Lieberman, A., eds. *Time to Learn.* Washington, D.C.: National Institute of Education, 1980.

Daft, Richard, and Becker, S. *The Innovative Organization.* New York: Elsevier, 1978.

Deal, Terrence, and Celotti, L. "Loose Coupling and the School Administrator: Some Recent Research Findings." Stanford: Stanford Center for Research and Development in Teaching, 1977.

Dewey, John. *Sources of Science Education.* New York: Liveright, 1979.

Dewey, John. *Experience and Education.* New York: Collier Books, 1963.

Gibbon, Peter. "Hartwick: Portrait of an Independent School." Doctoral dissertation, Teachers College, Columbia University, 1979.

Gross, Neal; Giacquinta, J.; and Bernstein, M. *Implementing Organizational Innovations.* New York: Basic Books, 1971.

Hall, Gene, and others. *Making Change Happen: A Case Study of School District Implementation.* Austin: Research and Development Center for Teacher Education, University of Texas, 1980.

Jackson, Philip. *Life in Classrooms.* New York: Holt, Rinehart & Winston, 1968.

Janesick, Valerie. "An Ethnographic Study of a Teacher's Classroom Perspective: Implications for Curriculum." East Lansing: Institute for Research on Teaching, Michigan State University, 1978.

Kepler, Karen. In *Time to Learn.* Edited by C. Denham and A. Lieberman. Washington, D.C.: National Institute of Education, 1980.

Lieberman, Ann. "The Effects of Principal Leadership on Teacher Morale, Professionalism, and Style in the Classroom." Doctoral dissertation, University of California at Los Angeles, 1969.

Lortie, Dan. *School Teacher.* Chicago: University of Chicago Press, 1975.

Maiocco, Don. "The Effects of Principal Leadership on Teacher Groups in Elementary Schools." Doctoral dissertation, Teachers College, Columbia University, 1977.

McLaughlin, Milbrey, and Marsh, D. "Staff Development and School Change." In *Staff Development, New Demands, New Realities.* Edited by A. Lieberman and L. Miller. New York: Teachers College Press, 1979.

McPherson, G. *Small Town Teacher.* Cambridge: Harvard University Press, 1972.

Meyer, John. "Notes on the Structure of Educational Organizations." Occasional

Paper #3. Stanford: Stanford Center for Research and Development in Teaching, 1975.

Miller, L., and Wolf, T. "Staff Development of School Change: Theory and Practice." In *Staff Development: New Demands, New Realities, New Perspectives.* Edited by A. Lieberman and L. Miller. New York: Teachers College Press, 1979.

Peltzman, Barbara. Doctoral dissertation. Teachers College, Columbia University, 1975.

Sarason, S. *The Creation of Settings and the Future Societies.* San Francisco: Jossey Bass, 1972.

Sarason, S. *The Culture of the School and the Problem of Change.* Boston: Allyn and Bacon, 1971.

Sarason, S. "The Nature of Problem Solving in Social Action." Address before the Eastern Psychological Association, Boston, 1977.

Sarason, Seymour; Levine, M.; and others. "Teaching is a Lonely Profession." In *Psychology in Community Settings: Clinical, Educational, Vocational, Social Aspects.* New York: John Wiley and Sons, 1966.

Smith, Louis, and Geoffrey, William. *Complexities of an Urban Classroom.* New York: Holt, Rinehart & Winston, 1968.

Smith, Louis, and Keith, P. *Anatomy of Educational Innovation.* New York: John Wiley and Sons, 1971.

Sussman, Leila. *Tales Out of School: Implementing Organization Change in the Elementary Grades.* Philadelphia: Temple University Press, 1977.

Waller, Willard. *Sociology of Teaching.* New York: John Wiley and Sons, 1967.

Weick, Karl. "Educational Organizations as Loosely Coupled Systems." *Administrative Science Quarterly* 21 (March 1976).

3

Life in Secondary Schools

Teachers' lives are shaped not only by their peculiar status as "professional adults" and purveyors of justice but also by the special quality of their work—a work that cannot be reduced to rules, competencies, techniques, or attitudes.

—Sara Lawrence Lightfoot, 1983

Life in secondary school is very different from life in elementary school. In this chapter we look at some of those differences, once again through the eyes of teachers. We also draw on our own field work in three specific high schools as well as the research and insights of other scholars and practitioners who are particularly sensitive to the world of high school teaching.[1] We have chosen three major themes to frame our discussion of high schools: (1) living in a bureaucracy, (2) working with adolescents, and (3) forging a faculty culture. Though not comprehensive, these three themes provide a basis for looking at high school teaching and making comparisons to the elementary setting. As in Chapter 2,

---

[1]The high schools we studied vary in size (from 1,200 to 3,000 students), in racial composition (from less than 1 percent minority to 20 percent and 70 percent), in location (Northeast inner-city, Northwest working class, Midwest small city), and in socioeconomic status (low, middle, and affluent). By secondary school, we refer specifically to schools that serve grades 9 through 12, although many middle schools are similar enough to these schools to warrant inclusion under this heading.

we aim to describe the social realities of teaching, to highlight major dilemmas, and to connect what we know about teaching with the implications of that knowledge for school improvement.

Living in a Bureaucracy

"I taught in elementary school for nine years before I was assigned to the high school as a resource room teacher. I can't adjust to the difference. The high school is like an armed camp with a complicated chain of command and enough rules and regulations to rival the army."*

More than the elementary school, the secondary school is a complex organization; it is more bureaucratic, more formal, and more difficult to negotiate. As such, the very organization of the school presents teachers with certain tensions that need resolution. The dilemmas or endemic uncertainties that secondary teachers face bear some similiarity to those that confront their elementary school counterparts. The bureaucratic nature of secondary schools, however, emphasizes some aspects of these common dilemmas and diminishes others.

Personal Control vs. Organizational Constraints

A high school teacher can close the classroom door and experience a large amount of autonomy and control in any building. However, secondary teachers must also deal with the larger school organization—its rules and regulations, its authority structure, its varied personnel, its policies and procedures—in a way that allows them to maintain the integrity of the classroom and to fulfill the often conflicting requirements of the school organization. Such is a reality of life in a bureaucracy.

As a bureaucracy, the school has a ladder of authority with the principal at the top rung, followed by the assistant principals, department heads, and, finally, by the teachers. Even at this bottom rung, there is a pecking order of sorts. Teachers are ranked by the number of years they have taught in a building and are often rewarded accordingly. The most experienced teachers may be assigned the "best" classes, while others spend the day working with the least desirable students, freshmen, sophomores, and non-college-bound students.

---

*All quotes from teachers are from field notes taken during 1979–80. The field study portion of this chapter was partially supported by NIE grant NIE-G-78-0184 at Northwestern University, Evanston, Illinois.

"I've been here five years, and finally I have been given one honors class to teach. These kids make my day; they're bright, alert, and motivated. I've always envied Mrs. B. for having all seniors and honors classes. I hang on, hoping that when she retires, I'll have my turn."

The result of this division of labor is that some amount of energy is spent among teachers jockeying for position within the informal hierarchy of each department as well as vying for the rewards that accrue to those who make their way up the career ladder in the formal hierarchy of the school.

In addition to the formal chain of command and the informal positioning among teachers, there is another structure of influences that intrudes on the lives of teachers in the complex organization of the secondary school. This includes positions that are not quite administrative and not quite teaching in nature and which reside outside the formal and informal power structures of the faculty. Such positions include guidance counselors, nurses, social workers, student activities directors, consultants, security guards, and custodians. Much to the chagrin of teachers, people in these positions often have authority that supersedes that of the faculty.

"The student activities director called a meeting of all girls wanting to play powder-puff football for the third hour today. Two hundred girls showed up for the meeting in the auditorium! Half of my class was missing. I had to completely alter my lesson plan for the day for a reason I consider utterly insane."

"A student was assigned to my honors calculus class who shouldn't even be in an advanced math. The counselor will not change his class for reasons I don't quite understand. So, now I have to teach one kind of math to 27 kids and another kind of math to one kid."

"I lock my door when the bell rings to discourage tardies. My plan is to keep them in the hall until I get the rest of the class working and then open the door for the tardies. The security guard saw the kids in the hall, knocked on my door, and told me I had to admit the kids because they were causing a nuisance."

High school teachers, then, find themselves in an unenviable position. Above them are all the people who have administrative authority; to the side of them are the nonteaching personnel who interfere with instructional and discipline plans. All seem to conspire to impinge on the teacher's control and autonomy in the classroom.

Secondary teachers are forced to deal with issues of the total school organization as well as with issues of the individual classroom. They must make adjustments in what they plan to do and how they do it; they must conform to a number of conditions that prevail in the building— conditions that are ever changing; they must acknowledge the influence structures of the school, formal and informal, and make their way around and through them; they must strike a delicate balance between individual wants and organizational needs.

The Dilemmas of Batch Processing

Life in high school is life in crowds, for both teachers and students. Because of the large number of students in any given high school, "batch processing" (Cusick, 1973) is the order of the day. So that students can be processed in batches, schools divide their days into discrete units of time for the purpose of distinct subject matter instruction. Students and teachers move through the building in mass, and they move every 50 minutes or so on the average of six times a day. Most teachers teach 125 to 150 students in a day. Most students meet with five teachers a day and with any number of students in separate classrooms. What are the effects of this method of processing large numbers of students? For one thing, it exhausts teachers.

"Most teachers here teach 25 hours per week. To someone who is not in education, this may seem to be a tremendously light schedule. However, if you are in education you understand that 25 hours of teaching means you have lots of hours in preparation for that to come off right."

"You don't have any time. That one period you have for preparation, you need for preparation. You also need it to interact with other teachers, to get out of your classroom, to get your head together, so to speak. It's a real exhausting day."

"From the time I enter the building until the time I leave, I'm in motion. In class you have to keep up and acting and moving. It's like a program in a way, not just a class."

Less able than elementary teachers to set their own pace over the course of a day, secondary teachers learn to accommodate to the rhythm the school imposes.

Batch processing has two other major effects on teachers: it requires them to take on a variety of noninstructional functions and, it largely determines one's mode of instruction. Noninstructional functions include all of those tasks that have to be accomplished for the maintenance of the school. Teachers have to monitor and record lateness and absence. Sometimes, the mere recording of this information takes ten to 15 minutes of instructional time per class hour (Miller, 1978). In addition to record keeping, teachers must assume responsibility for "duty" assignments, which usually involve supervision of corridors, lunchrooms, study halls, and parking lots.

> *"Most people think that what goes on in high school happens in the classroom. Well, they're wrong. It goes on in the corridors. Have you ever watched a passing period? It's incredible."*

The corridors are where a great deal of student life is focused; it is here that the social order of the school is most often threatened.

> *"You have all this action in the corridors. You need to be a strict disciplinarian. Teachers have to be on their toes. They can stop something before it starts; they can neutralize a situation."*

> *"You know, the corridors in these urban schools are a problem. You really need control, and the control needs to be consistent and has to be there all the time. The kids need to know this whether they like it or not."*

This recognition of the need for control places teachers in a contradictory position. On the one hand, they want to spend their time doing what they are trained to do, and that is to teach. On the other hand, in order for instruction to take place, order must be maintained. The teachers, then, become the police of the school. Most teachers view this role as a necessary evil; it "comes with the territory."

> *"The kids need to have order. They don't have anything to hold on to, and they need something to hang on to if they are going to learn anything."*

In a world where order precedes instruction, policing precedes teaching.

Batch processing not only influences what happens outside of classrooms; it has its effects on the instructional process itself. The typical 50-minute class period places a demand on the teacher to teach in a disjointed and rushed manner. Students enter one classroom after having spent time in another classroom with another teacher involved in another subject matter. As soon as students walk into the room, they are supposed to switch frames of reference. For teachers, a similar switch is necessary. Teachers are expected to put aside the concerns of the previous class and to concentrate on the one sitting in front of them at the present moment. The central concern for teachers in such a situation is . . .

". . . to keep within a time-frame, to keep the subject matter coherent, to keep it going in progressive patterns that make some kind of sense, and to have some time to summarize it for students at the end; to keep questioning them as you are introducing it to them to keep them on their toes. Also, to give yourself some feedback: are they really hearing this?"

Every teacher makes a separate peace with this concern. Because teaching is such a personalized and isolated activity, the solutions to shared problems are private solutions. For some, the solution is to keep things routine.

"The beginning of a class has a lot of routine involved in it. It is actually pretty boring. I would like to get a little more interesting materials to teach, but I don't want to risk it. It took me a long time to get into the groove that I'm in now."

For others, there are bursts of active enthusiasm and renewed commitments to do more and to do it better.

"I set a goal for my low-level kids. I wanted them to learn the times tables. Now, most people won't believe that a kid in high school can't multiply. I went to the store and bought some of those plastic times tables and gave them to them. I didn't tell them to shut off the TV or radio or to go in early at night. Just to keep the tables lying around the house—beside the TV, in the bedroom, in the bathroom. Look at them ten minutes a day; that's all. In class, we drilled and drilled. I made up games; I did everything to get them to learn those tables. I really got obsessed about it. By Thanksgiving, they all knew their tables. They felt terrific and I felt like a million dollars."

For most teachers, there is simply the need to get on with it, to pick up from where they left off yesterday and to prepare for what will happen tomorrow. Given the mass production quality of the school, what is important is keeping *on track* and keeping *in control*. Perhaps the most appropriate metaphor for high school teaching is a theatrical one.

"I see teaching as pure theatre. I think that all teachers are frustrated actors and the kids make such a good audience. It's a performance every day, a continuing soap opera, more than a one-shot performance. No two days are the same. Sometimes the performance is lousy. Some days you are up; some days you are down. Once in a while you give a command performance. But mostly, you just say to yourself, 'The show must go on.' "

The approach to teaching that one adopts is not necessarily the best one; it is the one that makes it possible to do what has to be done in the time allotted and under the conditions resulting from batch processing.

Tensions Surrounding Specialization

Question: What do you teach?
Elementary teacher: I teach children.
Secondary teacher: I teach math.

The question posed and its responses are part of the folklore that has developed about teaching. It is conventional wisdom that elementary teachers are child-focused and secondary teachers are subject matter-focused. Unlike the elementary teacher, the secondary teacher is a specialist—especially trained and licensed for the purpose of teaching a specific discipline. Almost all of the messages one receives as a secondary teacher, either in training or in practice, reinforce this subject matter orientation. Even the physical layout of most buildings makes distinctions by subject matter. There are corridors reserved for each of the teaching departments.

As a secondary teacher, one's identity is closely linked to the subject one teaches. "I'm an English teacher" connotes something different from, "I teach shop." One spends her life in the basement surrounded by heavy machinery and concrete materials; the other spends her time on the second floor surrounded by books and paper. So strong is subject matter compartmentalization that it is common for the shop teacher and the English teacher to never interact in the course of a school day, or in fact, in the course of a school year. This is all to say that in high school, what you teach is important; it is what you are.

As subject matter specialists, high school teachers see themselves as having higher status than elementary teachers.

"We have more academic training, more academic rigor than elementary teachers do. We have the potential to do more with our students."

But secondary teachers see themselves as having far less status than college professors, the ultimate subject matter specialists.

"There is academic competitiveness like an Olympic athlete. As a high school teacher, you only make the trials; you represent your country, but no one ever hears about you. In a way, in a heavy academic subject, if you're not way up then you're way down."

Lortie (1975) has discussed the relationship between high school and college teachers and refers to the position of the school teacher as being "special but shadowed." Secondary teachers, he says, "never did gain control of any area of practice where they were clearly in charge and most expert . . . Pedagogical theory and substantive expertise have been dominated by people in other roles" (page 12).

Secondary teachers, ever mindful of their precarious status as specialists, tend to approach teaching and learning in a way that is imitative of the "real" specialists. They depend on lecture and discussion techniques and focus on content more than on student effect.

The teachers' behavior in class is largely in keeping with their roles as experts. They set up their classes as dyadic interactions, they on one side and the students on the other. They then lecture, question, call on students to answer, pass out assignments, ask the students to read passages or paragraphs and then criticize and discuss their responses. Point by point, line by line, page by page, they pass on those pieces of knowledge that they consider important to their particular speciality (Cusick, 1973, p. 11).

Yet for many teachers, and their number is growing, this "didactic" approach to teaching is not working successfully. With no clear alternatives forthcoming and with no direction from anyone above them, secondary teachers continue to do what is most familiar. And they suffer the consequences in private.

Working With Adolescents

"They are a lost generation; they really are. They're separated, semi-adults. I think they come here frightened, and they feel lonely and confused. There are so many things going on in their lives, and we have to figure out ways to deal with them, to teach them something. It isn't easy."

Working with adolescents has never been easy. In recent years, the difficulties surrounding adolescence have been elevated to a national problem. While the experts convene in their task forces and blue-ribbon panels, pouring over data and making recommendations, secondary teachers are daily confronting the problem and devising their own solutions.

Starting at the End

The task of the secondary teacher begins at the end of a student's academic career in the public schools. By the time students reach high school, they have at least eight years experience with schooling. They have been tested, tracked, channeled, retested, and evaluated by a variety of educators in a variety of settings. Their academic fate has largely been determined.

"The problem with teaching in a high school is that by the time we get the kids, the damage is done. We have no way of knowing which kids have it and never used it and which kids never had it at all."

But no matter who walks through the classroom door, the secondary teacher has to figure out a way to teach him or her. The disparity among students is mammoth. Some enter high school with highly developed skills and successful school behaviors. Others have mastered the basics and, while not academically inspired, are willing to do what has to be done to graduate. Still others are quasi-literate, in need of basic skills development, motivation, and individual attention.

Teachers must make adjustments to deal with the wide range of students they teach. They have to raise and lower expectations for whole classes and for individuals within classes. They have to "cover" the same amount of material, but to different degrees of difficulty and sophistication for different students. They have to shift from abstract formal modes of teaching to those that are more concrete and immediate. They have to devise a system for evaluating students that is just and upholds standards. While all of this may be true for the elementary teacher, it is more problematic at the secondary level because of the academic history that students bring with them to school.

Confronting Personal Issues

Adolescents come to high school with personal histories as well. The current generation of secondary students probably has a wider range of life experiences than any other group of the same age in our history.

"These kids are awfully smart—in some sense. They know everything. There is very little that they haven't tried themselves or know someone who has—drugs, sex, you name it. It's almost as if you're standing in front of 30-year-olds, except they're kids. They're having babies and they're no more than babies themselves."

Secondary teachers can deal with the personal issues their students bring with them to class or they can choose to ignore anything but academic concerns. For those who cannot ignore the obvious pain and confusion that some students experience in and out of school, it is extremely difficult to figure out what to do to help. This is especially true for teachers who have been teaching for awhile and have firsthand knowledge of the contrast between this and past generations of students.

"I have just five years until I retire. I can't wait for the day to come. It's not that I don't like this business. It's just that I feel I've outlived my usefulness. I don't understand their lives, what they're into, why they do what they do. It used to be I could tell a kid in trouble what was right and what was wrong and what made sense. Now, there are so many of them with problems, and I feel that I have no good advice to give them."

Who am I? What can I offer to them? Why should they listen? These are the questions of a profession in crisis.

Teaching or Pastoral Care?

Perhaps the central dilemma for secondary teachers is deciding where to place one's emphasis in working with adolescents. The question becomes: am I primarily a teacher who is concerned with the mastery of academic content, or am I primarily a social worker of sorts concerned with the pastoral care of my students?

For those teachers who concentrate on teaching, there is a strong conviction that "in knowledge there is strength." There is also an acknowledgment that teaching one's subject is what one is trained to do, so one had better try to do it as well as possible. The point of reference for these teachers is clearly the subject matter.

"I went into high school teaching because I was excited about science. Even if they never use science in their lives, these kids should know some of what science offers them. They live in a technological age and I want them to be equipped to understand that age."

"I guess at some level I just want them to be exposed to what I love and what I teach. I want them to know somebody, even if they think I'm crazy, who's genuinely excited about history."

"I think we have to expose kids to things they don't get anywhere else. I took some kids to see Taming of the Shrew. *I know in my heart that some of them will never again see live theatre. I'm not sure they even liked the exposure, but I want them to have it. I want them to remember someday that they saw a live production of Shakespeare. I like to think they'll be enriched for the experience."*

Idealistic? Perhaps. But many teachers have had success with this.

Forging a Faculty Culture

"I think that in high school situations there is a need to come together during the day with people, even if it is only to laugh. I find that very necessary. I don't hang out with people to swap ideas; I do it to relax."

All teachers need a place to relax, a time to hide from students. Secondary teachers, unlike many elementary teachers, have that time built into the day through their scheduled "preparation" periods and free lunch hours. A unique faculty culture is forged during the time teachers spend together as part of the routine of the school day. One aspect of the culture is that it is composed of several subgroups. Such groups form along somewhat arbitrary lines: smokers, nonsmokers, men, women, academic teachers, vocational teachers, the vicissitudes of scheduling. These various groups are the basis of the faculty culture, which provides a special reference point for teachers—away from the formal demands of the bureaucracy and the tensions of dealing constantly with adolescents. The secondary school faculty culture is a haven for teachers. As such, the existence of this culture presents some major dilemmas for teachers to resolve.

The Dilemma of Identification

The faculty culture is the source of some rewards for teachers, freeing them from total dependence on the feedback of students. The culture also has its expectations, rules, norms, and sanctions—just as does any organization, formal or informal. Often, the rules underlying the faculty culture are in opposition to or co-exist with the rules of the formal school organization. Teachers have to decide how much of their organizational identity is attached to the bureaucracy of the school and how much derives from the informal peer culture.

For some teachers, the major source of identification is clearly the faculty culture, and the major stance they take *vis-a-vis* the school hierarchy is one of opposition. As an oppositional force, the faculty group spends a good deal of its time griping. The gripe session, in effect, becomes a stable interaction. In the gripe session, negative feelings about the school and about the students find an arena for expression with no expectation that problems will be resolved.

> *"It doesn't matter what the issue is, and lots of times it's a fake issue. It might be some bulletin the principal sent out or something a kid did in class. It's something we can find unanimity in. We can all agree, 'That's BAD,' and somehow that makes us feel good in comparison. It's never about anything you can do anything about."*

Griping is ritualized. It serves to build group identity and is a way to diminish feelings of isolation. Griping also tends to isolate teachers still further from administration and often from their students as well. Identification with the faculty culture is a double-edged sword. It offers the promise of a sense of belonging as an antidote to loneliness; it also offers potential for negativism and antagonism to any movement toward improvements that a school organization might undertake.

For other teachers, the identification with the faculty culture is important, though less intense. For them, a strong cohort group offers a reprieve from the hardships of teaching. It is a place where stories are exchanged and good-natured interactions encouraged. Though not involved in griping, these teachers take advantage of the group and take part in a form of verbal "jousting." In jousting, teachers may take a break from the classroom and unwind.

"We need a 'time out' from kids and classes and teaching. We need time to recharge for the next assault. We don't want to talk about anything serious. We want to take a break, kibitz, and then go back to our job."

Jousting can be seen as serious business. It is an effective way to ameliorate the tensions of work. Teachers who choose to participate in jousting and not in griping often strike a balance between fidelity to the school organization and fidelity to the faculty peer group.

For some teachers, there is a complete rejection of the peer group and a major identification with one's role as a teacher in the school. These faculty members are often "loners" who derive none of the benefits from participation in the faculty culture and who seek all of their rewards from their students. They are often disdainful of their colleagues, or they view identification with the faculty group as a hindrance to advancement in the school. They, like their cohorts, make a decision about their organizational identity and learn to live with the consequences.

Professional Engagement vs. Disengagement

The secondary school faculty culture is primarily a male culture; this is in marked contrast to the predominantly female environment of most elementary schools. As a male culture, the high school peer group deals with issues of career and professional engagement in ways that are quite different from what we find on the elementary level. As a result, the culture experiences a crisis of commitment.

The roots of this crisis can be found in the different career expectations of men and women teachers. The typical male teacher anticipates advancement to administrative ranks; the typical female teacher views classroom teaching as her life's work (Lortie, 1975). After ten or 15 years, many of the men who are still in the classroom have not fulfilled expectations; the women who are still teaching are more content. For men, teaching may become—in effect—a noncareer.

"I entered teaching thinking that I would teach five to seven years and take some courses to get my administrative license. By 30 or 35, I'd be assistant principal. In five years, I'd be a principal. Well, it obviously didn't work out as planned. I'm glad now; I have more time for other things."

Men who are still teaching at age 40 often develop outside activities, either avocations to which they are committed or additional employment that supplements their incomes and work lives. Disengagement from teaching becomes the norm.

The high school faculty, with its male majority, has to deal with issues of engagement and commitment in a way that is unique in public education. It is a decision that every teacher must make; its implications for the future of schooling and school improvements cannot be underestimated.

Implications for School Improvements

So far, we have dwelled on the descriptive aspects of life in high schools. We have tried to build a case for viewing secondary schools as complicated organizations, filled with unique contradictions and tensions. We have argued that these tensions make attempts at school improvement extremely difficult to initiate, support, and maintain. In the pages that follow, we turn our attention to the problem of improving secondary schools. We do not offer solutions; rather, we suggest possible strategies, highlight possibilities for intervention, and offer examples of approaches that have been effective in some specific settings. As a framework for our discussion, we depend on the categories of *social context, teachers, substance,* and *interpersonal relations* that were developed in Chapter 2. We are more concerned here about raising the right questions than we are about formulating the right answers.

Social Context

As with elementary schools, any effort to improve a specific secondary school must begin from a strong understanding about the social context of the school, both national and local. High schools today are very affected by the national climate; indeed, the major portion of the current debate on education concerns the high school curriculum. High schools are being told to have higher standards, more rigid graduation requirements, more science, more math, more foreign language—depending on what report one reads. In the 1980s, we should expect to see many changes and improvements in response to national concerns.

This is not to minimize the importance of local conditions. Like the elementary school, the high school must deal with the unique features of its district, its neighborhood, and its own culture. Some of the questions we may raise about the local context in regard to secondary school improvements are:

- *What is the general atmosphere of the school?*
  Do people identify with the school? Is there "school spirit"? How important are extracurricular concerns? Do people feel involved in or detached from the school? How do people view the school? Is it considered a "good" school? Who are the school's major champions? Who are the school's major critics? How much is the school affected by issues outside of it? To what extent is the school autonomous?

- *What is the nature of the student population?*
  Is the student population homogeneous or heterogeneous? What is the proportion between college-bound and non-college-bound students? Are teachers and students from similar or dissimilar backgrounds? Does the school have a large or small number of students who are considered "problem kids"? Has there been a stable or shifting student population over the past ten years? Is the student population predominantly urban or suburban? How would relations among the various student groups be characterized? Are some students considered more "teachable" than others? Who are they? By and large, how do students view the school?

- *What are local community expectations of the school?*
  What does the local community expect from the school in the way of preparation for the future? Does the community view the school as primarily college prep? As primarily pre-vocational? As a combination of both? Does the local community expect the school to be run as a "tight ship" with many rules and regulations or in a more open fashion with more responsibility placed on students? Are problems supposed to be solved within the school, or is it considered appropriate to use outside resources and agencies? Does the school receive much publicity? If so, what kind of publicity does it receive? Is the local community basically proud of the school?

- *How is power defined and allocated in the school?*
  Is power clearly vested in the formal hierarchy, or are there informal pockets of power within the school? Is there conflict among power sources? Who are the key brokers of power in the school? Is power vested in particular individuals or in small alliances?

Who in the school feels powerful enough to make changes and who does not? Is there a general feeling of potency in the school or a general feeling of impotence?

- *Is the school an orderly environment for teaching and learning?*
  Is the school orderly? Is the order in the school considered precarious or stable? Are rules and regulations enforced consistently? Are discipline concerns a major focus of the school? Are teachers called on to maintain order and control in nonclassroom settings? Are there many discipline referrals to the office, or are discipline issues handled primarily in the classroom? Do people in the school fear for their own personal safety? Or do people feel safe in school?

- *How is the school day structured?*
  What kind of schedule does the school use? How long are class periods? Does the schedule allow for double periods? Are there provisions in the schedule for team teaching? Does every teacher have his or her own room, or are there "floaters"? Are the various departments separated from each other or joined in some way? How are the rhythms of the school day characterized? Are there peak periods and low periods? Is instruction interrupted often, or are assemblies and other activities limited? How are teacher preparation periods assigned and used? Is the batch processing of students efficient or cumbersome?

The ways in which these questions are answered for each social context provide useful data for making decisions about how to initiate improvement efforts, with whom, and at what pace.

Teachers

We have noted that high school teachers differ from their elementary colleagues in a number of ways. They are specialists who see themselves as holding a position somewhere between the elementary teacher and the college professor; they are members of a unique faculty culture; and they tend to emphasize either subject matter concerns or issues involved in pastoral care. As we must learn to "read" the environment or social context of the school, so we must learn to "read" the faculty. In so doing, we may raise the following kinds of questions:

- *What are the major intellectual interests of the staff?*
  As "special but shadowed" professionals, secondary teachers never

quite fulfill their needs for intellectual pursuits. Any improvement effort on the high school level must approach teachers, first as specialists in their fields with intellectual interests and longing and, second, as teachers of adolescents with a vast store of insights and hunches about adolescent development. There are probably other intellectual interests as well; these need to be uncovered and legitimized. School improvements in high school should involve teachers as intellectuals and problem solvers and should draw on the accumulated knowledge of teachers as a major resource in all activities.

- *How may the faculty culture be characterized?*
  The faculty culture may be an active partner in school improvement efforts or a source of resistance. Much depends on the character of the culture itself and how that culture can become an arena for improvement activities. By assessing subgroupings of teachers, the norms of the groups, the leaders of the groups, and their stances *vis-a-vis* the organization, people concerned with school improvements can make decisions about who to involve first in any such efforts and how to make that involvement rewarded within the context of the faculty group. No school improvement can take place without active faculty involvement and support.

- *How do teachers view their mission?*
  In any high school, some teachers see themselves as transmitters of knowledge and others see themselves in social work kinds of roles. The degree to which a faculty adheres to either role definition is important data for school improvement. We have to ask teachers about their major concerns and then gear improvements towards meeting those concerns. An inaccurate assessment of a faculty can lead to failed efforts in any school.

Teachers are at the core of any improvement effort. We must pay particular attention to their needs, their longings, their personal and professional concerns, and the ways in which they function as a separate culture in the high school.

Substance

Substance, the actual content of the improvement, develops from what is known about the social context of a school and about its teachers. As we have noted earlier, in high school there is a fusing of instructional issues (what teachers do in classrooms) and organizational issues (how the school is operated). The substance of school improvements must attend to both levels of concern: the individual and the organizational. When we have decisions about the appropriate focus for school improvements, we are asking:

- *What ideas are most useful in individual classrooms?*
  What are the major instructional concerns of the teachers? Individualizing . . . grouping . . . testing . . . use of new methods . . . access to new knowledge about the subject matter? What are the most effective ways of teaching specific students? What new skills are necessary to deal with this new generation of adolescents? What are other teachers doing in their classrooms that might be applicable to mine?

- *What approaches or programs are most useful in addressing schoolwide issues?*
  Are there attendance or discipline policies that seem to work in situations similar to this one? What kinds of materials would best suit our students? How can space be used better? Are there scheduling and programming approaches that seem appropriate to the present situation? Are there alternative programs that might meet the needs of some of our students?

At root, questions about substance are questions about the utilization of knowledge; they are also questions about the adaptability of new ideas and approaches to the immediate environment. To the degree that school improvement efforts look to the context of the school and the needs and resources of the teachers for substantive issues, such improvements have a fair chance of getting a hearing and of being tried. The content of school improvements must emerge from the fabric of the school, its dailiness, and its people.

Interpersonal Relations Among School Personnel

We have focused some on the interactions among school personnel in our discussion of the faculty culture. Because of the size and scope of the high school, this faculty group remains the most pivotal force in the life of the school. This is not to say that principals and their relationship to staff members are not of major importance as well. Even in the largest buildings, the principal sets the tone.

"Under Mr. P. the school really worked. He went to all of the ball games; he was visible in the halls and in the classrooms. He supported teachers 100 percent. Now, with Mr. S. as principal, it's hard to believe that it's the same school. There's more chaos in the halls; teachers are demoralized; the building is a mess; it seems like nobody cares."

The principal in a high school affects faculty morale and can make or break any improvement effort.

High school principals approach their task either as leaders of instruction or as managers of operations. As a leader of instruction, the principal encourages instructional excellence, visits classrooms, talks with teachers about their teaching concerns, initiates program review and revitalization, is an active participant in the life of the school. Unfortunately, most high school principals do not approach their position this way. Rather they see themselves as managers of operations, people whose major concern is the smooth functioning of the building. By and large, managers spend more time in their office than in corridors and classrooms, attend numerous meetings outside of the building, remove themselves from the daily concerns of movement of students and life in classrooms, and establish social distance from the faculty.

"I see myself as the owner and manager of a medium-sized business more than as an educator. I have to make sure that the building works efficiently; that we meet all federal, state, and local guidelines; that we are in compliance with all laws. I'd like to have time for other things but I don't."

In terms of initiating and maintaining school improvements, the principal-as-leader is more likely to be involved than the principal-as-manager. Any improvement effort in the high school must begin with an understanding of the principal's definition of his or her role and how that definition affects the faculty. The principal cannot be ignored in a school improvement effort. If not actively involved, the principal must be kept informed and be supportive.

In addition to the principal and the teachers, we must pay attention to relationships among other certified and noncertified staff. We may ask:

- Do counselors and teachers work together or at cross-purposes?
- Do special teachers and consultants work with teachers in classrooms or in isolation?

- Do other school staff work with teachers in keeping order and control, or do they make their own policies?
- Do teachers feel supported in their work, or do they feel undermined?

By paying attention to the daily interactions and feelings that take place in a building, we are always gathering data about life in high schools. Such data, emerging as they do from the perceptions and understandings of the participants in an organization, provide the basis for sensitive and appropriate school improvement approaches at the high school level.

Case Studies

In concluding this chapter, we examine two high school improvement efforts that highlight issues of social context, teachers, substance, and interpersonal relations. We offer these two cases not as models to be replicated, but as examples for study and reflection. While there are no recipes for school improvements, we can use our accumulated practical knowledge and experience as a guidepost for action.

Big City High School

Big City High serves a student population of 2,200, of whom 60 percent are minority and 40 percent are white. The school is located in a city that has undergone a very long and painful court-mandated desegregation process. As part of the desegregation proposal, Big City was designated as a "magnet school" that could draw on students from the entire city in special areas. There have been three principals at Big City in five years' time. The faculty is relatively stable, having been at the same school for the past five years, since its opening.

The improvement effort at Big City involved the school faculty and its administration in collaboration with a nearby university. The effort was geared toward developing a variety of alternative programs in the school to serve the diverse student population. The major strategy was the establishment of a Teacher Center in the school building. The Center was initially headed by a university staff person; later leadership passed to a teacher at the school who was freed from classroom duties.

The Center became, over time, the meeting place for teachers who wanted to talk about educational issues and who wanted to plan for change in present structures and procedures. In effect, the Center became an alternative teachers' lounge. In the regular lounge, conversation continued in the "griping" and "jousting" vein. In the Teacher Center, conversation was of a more professional nature. Teachers could choose where they wanted to spend their preparation time. In the course of the school year, some 80 percent of the faculty had spent at least two preparation periods in the Center.

Among the accomplishments of teachers involved in the Center were the development of freshman and sophomore clusters, the establishment of a health-related program for volunteer students, the initiation of an in-school suspension program, and the review and revitalization of the school's math curriculum. Teachers came to the Center individually and in groups. They came to read, to reflect on their teaching, and to plan together. After three years, the Center is very much a part of the school. It has become an important school institution.

At Big City, the effect of the local context was minimal—even though other schools in the city were making national headlines for disruptions. The emphasis was on the teachers and the social world they inhabited while at school. Interpersonal relationships were stressed as new teams were formed and new alliances cemented. The substance of the improvement strategy was derived from the needs of the students and centered on program and curriculum development. The role of the principal was significant in the first year. In the second and third year, a different principal was in charge of the building, and his involvement in the Center was minimal. He did, however, lend support to the teachers and help them implement their new programs by adjusting the school schedule accordingly. He also supported the Center by allowing a teacher to have release time and serve as the director of the Center.

Mid City High School

Mid City High School serves a student population of 1,200, of whom 80 percent are white and 20 percent are black. The school draws on the richest and the poorest sections of the middle-sized city in which it is located. Five years earlier, the school was combined with another local high school. There is still some evidence of rivalry between the faculty and the communities of the schools involved in the merger. Mid City is located in a city that is undergoing voluntary desegregation. A new superintendent was brought in to oversee the desegregation process and to upgrade the quality of the city's schools. One of his first acts was to re-assign 80 percent of the principals and assistant principals in the district. This affected Mid City severely, since prior to the districtwide transfers, its long-time principal had been fired. The school has had three principals in less than six months. The new administrative team consists of a principal who had for 12 years previously been assigned to a quasi-suburban high school serving a predominantly white student body, an assistant principal with some 25 years experience in the system and who is now the only remaining administrator at the school, and another assistant principal new to the area and to the school system. The faculty consists of 66 full-time people, many of whom may not be at the high school the following year due to a nearly approved reassignment process for teachers based on seniority. In the year to come, the school population will increase to 1,725 students when the 9th grade will be added to the school.

The improvement strategy was initiated by the administrative team in the building. A faculty/administrative steering committee for "Quality Integrated Education" was named. The committee asked teachers to volunteer to serve on a variety of task forces, each aimed at offering alternative solutions for problems the school would face in the next school year. Teachers joined task forces that met during their preparation periods twice a month. Task forces focused on attendance, discipline, materials, scheduling and planning, professional development, gifted and talented programming, staff relations, noncertified staff issues, dealing with the freshmen, evaluation and grading, student activities and athletics, and staff-student concerns. As task forces made suggestions, the steering committee met to assess their viability and make recommendations for policy in the school.

At Mid City, unlike Big City, the effects of the larger social context dominated the life of the school. Teachers and students were concerned about their assignments for the coming year; staff members were preparing to teach more and younger students than they had before; administrators were being carefully watched by their immediate supervisors and lived in fear of yet another surprise transfer. The improvement strategy at Mid City developed around the issues that the local context was posing, issues of reorganization and radical change in student populations. These issues became the substance of the improvement effort. Interpersonal relations were central to the approach as teachers began meeting in groups to study problems and offer solutions. Teachers depended on each other and their shared experiences in facing many of the issues raised.

Unfortunately, what seemed like a full-scale improvement strategy didn't work. The principal, while initially supportive of teacher involvement, became resistant to instituting changes when the recommended changes were viewed as challenges to his management style. The conditions in the immediate environment of the school deteriorated. Students were spending time outside the building and on nearby streets in flagrant violation of the school's efforts to impose a harsher discipline code. The general morale of the school district continued to decline as more principals feared transfer and teachers readied themselves for another set of negotiations about reduction in force. All of these factors contributed to a failed change effort.

Both of these cases highlight the importance of attending to social context, the teachers, the substance, and the interpersonal relationships in designing and implementing an improvement strategy. In our first case, the strategy for school improvement was successful because it developed from the social realities of Big City High. It drew on the talents and skills of the teachers involved and it had the support of the principal. Over time, the Teacher Center became incorporated into the life of the school. In the second case, the strategy failed because it never penetrated the culture of Mid City High. A fearful principal blocked, rather than encouraged, change. Teachers withdrew their involvement and support; the social environment of the school deteriorated quickly. If these two cases teach us anything, it is that *planning* for school improvement is not sufficient. A plan has to earn acceptance and become incorporated into the routines of the school if it is to succeed. Such acceptance and incorporation develop over time and depend on a fine interplay among context, substance, teachers, and staff members' interactions with each other and with the change itself.

References

Cusick, Philip A. *Inside High School.* New York: Holt, Rinehart & Winston, 1973.
Lightfoot, Sara Lawrence. "The Lives of Teachers." In *Handbook of Teaching and Policy.* Edited by L.S. Shulman and G. Sykes. New York: Longman, 1983.
Lortie, Dan. *School Teacher.* Chicago: University of Chicago Press, 1975.
Miller, Lynne. "Non-Instructional Class Time." Unpublished study, 1978.
Smith, L., and Keith, P. *Anatomy of Educational Innovation.* New York: John Wiley and Sons, 1971.

4

School Leadership: There is No Magic

It is not the teachers, or the central office people, or the university people who are really causing schools to be the way they are or changing the way they might be. It is whoever lives in the principal's office.

—Roland Barth, 1976

Through our discussions of teaching and schooling, one figure looms large—albeit sometimes from the shadows. The school principal, no matter what his or her background abilities, is someone who must be reckoned with in efforts to make schools better. Current studies (Berman and McLaughlin, 1978) tell us again and again that the principal is the critical person in school improvement, that building level leadership is the single most important variable in changing an emphasis, setting a tone, implementing a program, opening or closing a possibility.

And yet, our knowledge about school leadership is sparse. With a few notable exceptions (Wolcott, 1973; Barth, 1980) we have little in the way of description about what it is that principals do and how they do it. In the pages that follow, we begin to chart those untried waters. Drawing again on our knowledge of "the field," we first describe and then analyze the social realities of leadership in a school.

A Week in the Life. . . .

For the last ten or twenty years, people have been trying to influence what happens in schools by riding in on white horses, carrying the latest curriculum unit or the latest philosophy of education, and then charging off. What they discovered—and it came as a shock—was that they had to live under the roof of the school to have an influence on it—and even then, change was not assured (Barth, 1976).

Two years ago, Lynne Miller had the opportunity to "live under the roof" of a school as a building administrator. With a background in leadership theory, understandings about improvement processes, and recent experience as a staff developer, she was hired—in the words of the superintendent—"to see whether all that theory can actually be applied to a school and have any impact." Like most entry-level administrators, her assignment was as an assistant principal in a high school, referred to here as Albion High School.

Located in a medium sized city, Albion is one of five high schools in a metropolitan area with a student population of 25,000. Albion comes as close as possible to being a "typical American high school." With a student population of 1,700 in grades 9–12, the school draws on a wide range of the city's population. Its 25 percent minority enrollment represents the city's population. The students are, by and large, well socialized; there is a sense of "school spirit" and high attendance at varsity sports events. A small group of students—at the very top of their classes—earn national honors and scholarships and are admitted to nationally recognized colleges and universities. Another small group of students—those at the bottom of the heap—are disaffected and spend a large part of their time hanging outside the building or "cruising" around in their cars. The majority of the students are law-abiding, regular-attending students with some intellectual interest in their studies who manage to do what has to be done to pass their classes, graduate, and go off to local colleges or jobs.

The staff of Albion is mostly middle-aged with an average of 20 years of teaching experience. Teachers have an active professional association, which just recently negotiated a very attractive contract, a model for the state. There is little antagonism between building administrators and teaching staff. Teachers take pride in their work, and one can still hear conversations that concern professionalism.

Though usually associated with school discipline, the role of the assistant principal varies from school to school. At Albion, the three administrators work as an administrative team with shared responsibilities and areas of specific control and supervision. There is no doubt that the principal has the final word on decisions and is ultimately in charge of the school, though the assistant principals have opportunity for assuming a good deal of school leadership and administration. By presenting a week in the life of one assistant principal, we hope to capture some of the flavor of the job and to point out some of the potential for establishing positive leadership, as well as the difficulties in being the kind of principal who can really make a difference in a school. Our narrative is told in the first person and is developed from daily notes taken the first year on the job. The week described occurs sometime in late winter/early spring.

Monday

The day begins as usual. I arrive about 7:30, check in with my secretary, other administrators, and office staff. By 7:45 I am on the third floor, enforcing the "8:00 rule," which stipulates that no students go beyond the first floor until 8:00. Enforcement had been lax until a fire, which was classified as arson, broke out on a third-floor corridor; since then, we have made sure that no students are unsupervised early in the morning.

I've come to enjoy these 15 minutes at the beginning of school. It gives me time to chat with students and teachers. There is a lot of good-natured kidding about "not until 8:00," and the students are cooperative and sometimes actually helpful.

The first agenda item for the morning, since it is Monday, is the administration/guidance meeting. The idea of this meeting is to create a "team" feeling among counselors and principals. Somehow, after several months of trying, this just isn't working. The meeting is marked by silences, false starts, and disengagement. I think we're all about to give up on the idea. It sounded fine on paper, but it didn't work out as intended.

This is the week I am scheduled to have conferences and class observations with teachers as part of the school system's new evaluation procedure. I want to take this part of my job seriously and apply all of my training in supervision, but time is short and commitment low. My first conference is with Mr. Smith. Despite constant phone interruptions and knocks on my office door, we manage to arrange a time for an observation. Mr. Smith says he doesn't want me to look at anything special—just to observe in general.

In the outer office I find two students who have been expelled from Mrs. Garvin's class for "gross insubordination," one of those vague terms that gets bandied about on discipline forms. It usually means that a student talked back to a teacher. I speak to the two offenders and get their side of the story and set up a time tomorrow for a conference with them and Mrs. Garvin so that we can talk this out. Mrs. Garvin makes a large number of student referrals, and I have found that a student/teacher conference is the best response.

People step in and out of my office to chat, register complaints, or make suggestions. As the bell rings for the changing of each class, I make it a point to drop what I am doing and make myself visible in the halls. I try to be on each of the three floors sometime during the day and usually hang around until after the tardy bell has sounded to watch stragglers get to class. We have three security guards, but I find that my own presence in the hallways is appreciated by staff and students.

I try to steal a half hour before lunch to work on an enrollment report that is due on Wednesday. It's a simple but time-consuming form. When it becomes obvious that I won't have the quiet I need to complete the form, I put it aside and vow to complete it before I leave the building this afternoon.

Lunch hour, actually 90 minutes, begins. We have to get three shifts in and out, which is no mean feat. Today there are no incidents in the lunchroom; the school feels calm. Someone says that the barometric pressure is steady, which accounts for the relative quiet of the building. I catch myself almost believing it.

The afternoon slips by. I have one more teacher conference in preparation for an observation. Again, I don't feel effective as a clinical supervisor. Is it the process, or is it me?

I meet with two people from the local university about our getting involved in a labor history project; they want our teachers to use their resources. I promise to set up a meeting with two history teachers who might be sympathetic, though I give no assurances. Our social studies department has not been particularly receptive to my overtures, but I will give it a try.

The dismissal bell rings and the building clears of students. My desk, orderly in the morning, now looks like a disaster area. The state enrollment report sits, unfinished, on top of the pile on my desk. I glance at it as I get involved in a conversation with two teachers about how today's adolescents differ from their predecessors. The conversation lasts until about 4:00. I'll get to the enrollment report tomorrow.

Tuesday

I begin, as usual, with the third-floor monitoring. I make it to my office in time for the promised teacher/pupil conference. True to form, Mrs. Garvin gives a brief lecture to the two boys about appropriate classroom behavior and asks them if they are ready to return to class. The boys nod silently in assent and then are dismissed. I say nothing yet wonder, as I always do, just why Mrs. Garvin considers my presence at these meetings so important. Perhaps it is just my presence that does it for her, knowing there is someone watching her as she tries to get through to some students.

Two other students, among our honors kids, come by to report a locker break-in. They are almost strident in their call for stalking out suspects and bringing them to justice. Against my better judgment, I find myself engaged in a somewhat heated discussion, trying to get them to look at their most basic assumptions about why some kids steal from others. The bell rings and we agree to continue this discussion later.

I manage to spend a full hour observing Mr. Clarke in chemistry. He is a gifted teacher. What is there to say to him when the class is dismissed except, "Good work; keep it up"? And that about takes care of the all-important post-conference. I think Mr. Clarke is a good teacher and he knows it. I feel silly saying anything more. He accepts the compliment and then thanks me for the positive reinforcement.

I remember to call the computer center downtown about next semester's scheduling and to begin my meetings with department chairs about next year's budget. We are going to be cut across the board, and the departments are going to have to make necessary adjustments. Actually, the principal deals with all budget matters, but since I am eager to learn all aspects of administering a school, I sit in on these discussions. There is another aspect of administering a high school that I am less interested in, though it seems to have major importance, and that is the handling of athletics. The athletic program takes considerable time in a high school principal's schedule. There are biweekly meetings to attend, budgets to adjust, appearances to be made. In our district, principals are often judged by the degree of their involvement in their schools' athletic programs.

Back in my office I find a small mountain of phone messages: some from parents, some from other administrators, one from the juvenile office, and one from the director of administration reminding me that the enrollment report is due tomorrow. As I get ready to answer the messages before me, seven students enter my office. They have come to complain about a teacher, Mr. Carr. This is not the first time a student or a parent has registered such a complaint. I have met with Mr. Carr several times and have literally gotten nowhere. The issues this time are unclear directions about assignments, no reporting of grades, discrimination against some students, and favoritism toward others. I listen to the students, tell them I appreciate their concern and that I will investigate this further. I also direct them to keep attending class, but I realize that I'm at a loss about what to do. All of my clinical supervision skills have failed me. I confer with the principal, and we decide to meet with Mr. Carr together and see how far we can get with him.

Lunch hour is a pleasant respite. I eat with a group of students who serve as peer counselors. The conversation is lively and energizing.

A conflict erupts in the cafeteria between ten black students and the two white lunchroom supervisors. It seems that the supervisors had asked the boys to turn off their radios. They pointed to several white students with radios and said, "Not until they turn off theirs." This is another example, I assume, of gross insubordination. The two teachers in charge were livid, demanding five-day suspensions for the youngsters. A quick look around the room indicates that there are, in fact, several white kids with radios. I solicit the help of a counselor, and we ask each group to lower their radios. Everyone complies; an incident is averted—for now. I feel like I'm knee-deep in personal and institutional racism, and I'm not sure what to do. This is an issue that needs addressing by the whole staff. I leave the cafeteria trying to figure out how to best tackle this problem.

In the hallway, I run into a teacher I know quite well. We talk about the lunchroom incident, and he tells me that it is not a new occurrence and sympathizes with my predicament. In effect, he gives me a "pep talk," encouraging me to keep up the fight. I realize how much I need some reinforcement, too.

As I walk down the hall at class passing time, I get into a conversation with an English teacher who is trying a new language game in her class. She invites me to visit. I enjoy the class and end up participating in it. When the period ends, the teacher is very excited, and we talk about all that happened, exchanging insights and suggestions for improvements. This feels like real supervision and instructional assistance.

I head for my office, only to find my secretary in a panic. Where was I? People have been in and out looking for me. Next time, tell her exactly where I'll be, please.

Mr. Lowry is waiting in my office. Sitting across from him is Joe Shepard, glowering. These two are at it again. Mr. Lowry begins, "Joe has been insubordinate. I won't have him in my classroom. He shouted obscenities at me. I won't stand for it." Exit Mr. Lowry. I turn to Joe. "I did yell at him, but I'm human, too." I know enough about Joe and Mr. Lowry to know that Joe is as much in the right (or wrong) as Lowry. I arrange to have Joe meet with me every day during the class time and complete lessons supplied by Lowry. By next week, things will cool down, and Lowry and Joe will be able to live in the same classroom again. I make a note to observe Lowry and have a long conference.

Finally, the day is at its end. Except for the enrollment report, all that has to be done is done. I vow to complete the report before I leave my office again.

Wednesday

I get to the third floor ten minutes late—too late. Two teachers and a student are battling. Seems the student, Linda Foley, had come up to her class before 8:00 to meet with her teacher, who was late. Linda was caught violating the "8:00 rule" and was busily defending herself when I arrived. Her defense was not appreciated by the apprehending teachers. Her language was laced with choice epithets, and the teachers were livid, demanding harsh disciplinary action. I had Linda go to my office, where I later found her in tears. The teacher with whom she had the early morning appointment was there also, taking Linda's side. She thought that the other teachers had acted too precipitously and come down too hard on Linda. I sent Linda home for the day, not as a suspension, but to cool down. This was a solution that Linda, the teacher, and I could live with. Linda went, on her own, to apologize to the teachers she had insulted. I feel that while we can't condone abusive language on the part of students, there is no use in punishing a student who has already punished herself and made her own apologies. This solution, so rational to me, does not sit well with the teachers involved. One even calls the superintendent to demand harsher discipline for students. I spend a good deal of time talking to the teachers, explaining my rationale, but to no avail. I know that it takes time to work through these issues, but my perspective is suddenly very short-range and so is theirs. There is to be no easy reconciliation here.

The day goes from bad to worse. There is a fight in the second-floor hall and another one in the first-floor girls' room. The offending students—all of them—are suspended until their parents come in for a conference. When I started this job, I vowed I would never suspend any student for any reason. I now use suspension very selectively, usually in cases like this where there is physical violence. I discover that I have made keeping the school a safe and secure environment one of my top priorities.

Two more classroom observations, no more satisfying than the others. Time is short; teachers are tense. Perhaps at a later time, we'll be able to talk about what happened in the classroom.

One of the teachers on the American history team invites me to attend a class. He has heard about the day's disruptions and offers me some comfort within the walls of his classroom. The class is simply spectacular. The students are in the midst of trying some robber barons for their crimes. I watch students who are apathetic in other classes come to life here and participate. There is genuine enthusiasm as each group of students builds its case. The class passes quickly. After the bell, I spend about half an hour with the two team teachers, and we carefully review all that went on. My input is solicited and valued. "Sometimes we're so close, we don't see things," they say. I must confess to myself that this is an example of good supervision and instructional assistance. It happens when trust has been established, and it happens in spontaneous ways. I decide to spend more time cultivating this kind of relationship with teachers, even as I go about the required structured observations.

I return to my office to get my desk in order—a losing battle. I then return a phone call from a parent who wants to complain about the practice schedule of the baseball team, and check in with the other principals and counselors to see whether there is anything I've missed that I should know about. The day ends more quietly than it began. On the way out, a teacher tells me that the barometric pressure was very high today. That accounts for it, I think, as I leave the building.

Thursday

All quiet on the third floor. I find out that teachers are split about yesterday's incident. It's been a heated topic of conversation.

Today is the day that the principal and I meet with Mr. Carr. I have accumulated a file of student and parent complaints and a record of conferences I have had with Mr. Carr. The principal opens the conference by saying he wants us to meet so that we can help Mr. Carr figure out ways to deal with his classes that are more satisfying to him and his students. "Help" was the wrong word. "Help? I don't need help. I've been teaching for 30 years. I don't need help. The students have lost all respect. Discipline has fallen down. I need support from you in dealing with students, not help. Check all my previous evaluations. All are satisfactory or excellent. This is the first year I have ever had any complaints. No one ever said anything to me before that even suggested I need help." The principal tries again. He notes the specific complaints about unclear assignments, lack of grades, discrimination, and favoritism. Mr. Carr brings out his gradebook and shows all sorts of grades. He counters the other charges by claiming that he makes demands on students to achieve; since the students aren't used to this, they rebel. The principal and I make some specific suggestions about informing parents and students about procedures in the class. The tension is diffused. The conference ends with Mr. Carr thanking us for listening to him.

Now, by most standards in the school, the conference is a success. There are minimal hard feelings; all charges have been addressed; a plan of action has been suggested; and the teacher feels better and even supported. In the end, nothing has really happened. A quick check of past evaluations shows that Mr. Carr's assessment is accurate. No one has ever suggested to him in a formal way that his teaching can be improved. And yet, the general gossip around the school has Mr. Carr typed as a less than competent teacher. Generations of students and their parents have lobbied with the counselors to remove names from his class rolls before the first day of school. All of this has taken place in informal ways, and Mr. Carr continues to teach, unchallenged. But what of the students in his classes? That's a question I can't answer immediately. I make it a point to pay more visits to Mr. Carr's class and to document all that I see. I also decide to talk to him more regularly about what is going on. In time, one of two alternatives will be taken: either Mr. Carr will work to improve his teaching with "help" from administrators and the department chair, or we will have gathered enough information to place him on probation, at which point a formal "instructional assistance team" will be assigned to him.

I move from one conference to another. This one is with the parents of one of the students involved in fights yesterday. The conference takes some time. First the parents vent steam at the school, then at their child, and finally turn inward and blame themselves. We talk for awhile and decide to explore some general counseling for the whole family. The fight at school is symptomatic of other, deeper issues. The student returns to class, and the parents and I agree to talk on the phone regularly.

I take my usual hourly stroll of the building and peek into the speech and debate class, where the new topic is on improving education. The students ask me a great deal of questions and strike a deal with me whereby they can have access to my personal library. I know these kids well, since I judge debate and speech competitions on weekends. I do this as a gesture in support of Mrs. Kinney, who every weekend packs ten to 15 kids into a van and drives them all over the state to compete with other debaters. She receives no compensation for this. A veritable "Mrs. Chips."

From the sublime to the mundane. I move from a stimulating hour with the debate team to a long discussion with the sponsors of the cheerleading and pom-pom squads. The reluctant sponsor talks about the harms of "tokenism" and the horrors of "compromising standards." Finally I say, "Elaine, I want one minority girl on varsity and one on junior varsity—at the very minimum." "Is that an administrative directive?" she asks. "Yes," I reply. So much for democratic decision making and responsive leadership.

The rest of the day goes without incident. I make the usual rounds, talk to teachers and students, hold impromptu conferences and formal observations, and attack my desk one last time. Finally, it's time for dismissal. Since it's Thursday, there is always the possibility that a schoolwide or departmental meeting is scheduled. Today, the English department is meeting about rethinking the general (lowest track) curriculum. This particular group has been meeting for the last month. It is now a convivial group, after some early dissension and defensiveness.

After socializing, we get down to the task and begin discussing perceptions of the general student. We decide to begin a collective resource file of exercises, lesson plans, and ideas that work for general students. Each teacher is to contribute materials, and sometime during the summer the department head and I will sort things out and begin the file. We also decide to provide each teacher with the most recent reading scores of all students, assuming that such information will shock some teachers into modifying their teaching. The meeting goes on until 4:45 and then peters out. We all head for home.

Friday

Today is the second round of the basketball sectional. By some quirk of fate, our somewhat mediocre team now has a chance of taking the city title. A pep rally has been planned since early in the week. Pep assemblies are one of those issues that divides the faculty down the middle. Some think them essential for building "school spirit," and others see them as a waste of precious instructional time. We have compromised by planning an assembly that takes precisely 55 minutes. (In previous years, pep assemblies lasted as long as three hours and then school was dismissed early.) All goes as planned. The cheerleaders cheer; the pom-pom girls do their routine; the band plays loudly and well; the coach speaks; the team is introduced; the students shout and cheer. It is all over in the prescribed 55 minutes. There are no disruptions. Even the most cynical of the faculty comment on the efficiency of the operation. We stress that it will be "business as usual" the rest of the day.

Business as usual it is. Two observational post-conferences, one satisfying, the other less so. Hourly strolls through the halls. The usual barrage of phone calls. Talk of the game that evening. (I will have to attend and help supervise.) One last assault on my desk. I will clear it before I leave today, to make a fresh start on Monday. The school mail brings my paycheck and yet another report to be completed. The dismissal bell rings. All of us—students, teachers, administrators—beat a fast path home.

Reflecting on Experience: Conceptualizing a Role

Social scientists and practical men (sic) of affairs are intrigued by the phenomenon of leadership. Yet, despite a considerable body of speculative and scientific writing on its meaning, its determinants, and its effects, our knowlegde of the nature and correlates of leadership remain quite limited (Gross and Herriott, 1965).

As our description of a week in the life of a school administrator suggests, principaling is a lot like teaching. It is personal, conflictual, and uncertain. One learns the job by doing it, never sure that the job is being done well. More artist than scientist, the principal works—through trial and error, intuition and experience—to make sense of the role and to lead others through a precarious institution. But a question remains: what are the unique "nature and correlates" of the position of principal? What qualities of mind, aspects of personality, behaviors, attitudes, skills, and propensities contribute to the playing of the role? What, in fact, does being a principal entail? We view the principalship as not one role, but many roles. We find it useful to discuss these roles in clusters of behaviors and expectations: (1) those that deal primarily with interactions, (2) those that focus on management, and (3) those that center on leadership. Following, we present each cluster and the different roles that fall within each.

For let no one be deceived, the important things that happen in schools result from the interactions of personalities (Waller, 1932).

Omniscient Overseer

A principal simply has to know everything that is happening in the building all of the time. While teachers focus on the particular, principals look to the general—not one classroom, but all classrooms; not one interaction, but all interactions. The principal's concern includes the physical plant, social organization, the curriculum, and the extra-curriculum, the larger community. Everything that happens in a building becomes important—a leaky faucet, a disorderly class, a complaining parent, an incompetent teacher, a schedule change, a faulty circuit, a faulty curriculum. The view from the principal's office has to be broad and clear; it must encompass everything.

Confidant and Keeper of Secrets

The principal gains knowledge of the school through a variety of sources, some public, some private.

As the key communication links in their organization, administrators know much that they cannot share with others. These confidential matters, be they good or bad secrets, are an important part of administrative life (Burlingame, 1979).

Keeping secrets means isolation. It means having the fortitude not to share knowledge about a particular teacher, a particular incident, a particular problem that needs solving in private. The confidences of students about their classes, a teacher's inability to keep class control, underlying currents of hostility that threaten to flare up at a moment's notice—these are the secrets a principal keeps. They are private matters in a very public world.

Sifter and Sorter of Knowledge

One of the problems about knowing everything is that all things can seem equally important. The principal has to make distinctions and has to decide what needs attending and in what order. Is cheerleader selection more or less important than attending a department curriculum meeting? Does enforcement of the "8:00 rule" take precedence over students having access to teachers before school? What has top priority: completing a state form on time or meeting with a teacher in distress? Which tasks can be delegated and which ones require personal attention? Such are the distinctions a principal must make, under conditions that are less than ideal, again and again in the course of a day, a week, a term, a year.

Pace-Setter and Routinizer

There is periodicity of life in schools; much of the school's regularity is set by the principal. Again drawing on our description of an administrator's week, there is the Monday guidance meeting, the Thursday voluntary teachers meetings, the daily monitoring of the third-floor corridor before school, the hourly promenade through the halls at the passing of classes, the informal sessions over coffee, the "open door" at the end of the day. Small rituals that help give order to a school. As routines are established, expectations are fixed. The routines of an administrator lend stability to a building as the routines of a teacher stabilize a classroom.

Referee

A principal spends a good part of the work day running interference between groups and individuals who are in conflict, acting as a referee in a game where the rules are unclear. Whether intervening in Mrs. Gavin's class expulsions, the lunchroom radio crisis, Linda's use of expletives, or Joe Shepard's plea for humane treatment, the principal is there as an arbiter of fair play. On another level, the principal referees between department chairs covetous of classroom space or a large share of the budget, having to mediate between the faculty advocates of "school spirit" and those who favor uninterrupted instruction. Daily, the principal stands at the center of an arena of dissenting factions, sure to offend someone and to never please everyone.

Linker and Broker

Principals link people, ideas, resources within and outside of the school building. They know the needs and skills of the faculty and are able to make good matches, if they take the time to do so. In the larger world of the district and the community, principals broker with the central office, outside agencies, and local authorities to gain services and recognition for their schools. Perhaps more than anyone else on the staff, the principal is cosmopolitan—using connections to make the school a richer place. Introducing a university-based labor history project, making referrals to county mental health agencies, keeping in touch with the juvenile division of the police, being in close contact with the decision makers downtown—all of these activities help cement alliances that affect the smooth functioning of the school.

Translator and Transformer

As the school's chief executive, the principal has to carry out policy from above as well as make policy from within. A principal receives an order from his or her supervisor, a central office administrator who has long been out of touch with schools. Be it a new teacher evaluation procedure, a revised discipline code, a scheduling format change—all such policies are left to the principal to translate to staff members and to transform to meet the needs of a particular building at a particular time. What is actually implemented looks little like what has been mandated; it is re-formed to fit the mold of the school. The policy seldom reshapes the school; the school reshapes the policy (Berman and McLaughlin, 1978). And it is the principal who is the primary architect of the project. Whatever his motivations for seeking the position, they do not include being a housekeeper, a highly paid clerk, or embattled figurehead (Sarason, 1971).

Paper Pusher, Accountant, Clerk

Principals are overwhelmed with housekeeping responsibilities. With new legislative mandates, local accountability procedures, and specially targeted programs there are new forms to complete, new numbers to tally, new reports to file, new records to organize. The teacher evaluation procedure at Albion required documented observational notes as well as a narrative summary. Because the material was confidential, the three principals did their own typing, duplicating, and mailing of the forms for every teacher in the school. The state enrollment report that hung like an albatross around the neck of the assistant principal was one of many time-consuming bits of paperwork. In addition, there were a budget to develop, space to allocate, schedules to program, and a desk constantly in need of clearing. Unlike their counterparts in industry, principals do not supervise over rationalized operations. There is still a quality of "Bartleby, the Scrivener" to the school office.

Some principals become "good office people," venturing out into the school on rare occasions. For them, there is some joy in all the paperwork.

Retreating to the desk allows information gathering to occur in private, peaceful surroundings without the potential dramas that inevitably stalk the principal. In an intensely interpersonal world in which nothing ever seems constant, the "In" and "Out" baskets are comfortable markers of tangible success (Burlingame, 1979).

Others view housekeeping and clerical chores as sources of annoyance and pain. The work gets done, but it is done on overtime. There are no rewards for putting other concerns first.

Plant Manager

No matter how else they construe their role, principals are ultimately accountable for the smooth operation of their building. They are managers of all resources—material and human. Their job is to "maintain order, maximize production, and minimize dissonance" (Barth, 1981). They represent "management" and the teachers represent "labor." They supervise a staff that includes a teaching faculty, custodians and engineers, and cafeteria workers. If the building is in disarray or the grounds unkempt or the cafeteria service inefficient, it is the principal's job to put things back in working order. A public measure of a principal's competence is the well-functioning of the plant. It is an area that requires careful and constant scrutiny and immediate action to put things aright.

Disciplinarian

Part of maintaining a plant is maintaining order. Whether or not responsibility for enforcing discipline is delegated, the principal sets a tone for what is expected, what is tolerated, and what is punished. A school has a reputation as "loose" or as being a "tight ship," and it rests on the principal to make that reputation. The staff follows the principal's lead. At some schools, there are general parameters of appropriate behavior; Albion follows this model. At other schools, there are a plethora of rules and regulations and a specified response for each infraction. Teachers watch and wait to see how discipline is handled in the executive office and then follow suit in their individual classrooms. Principals are seen as weak or strong based on how they view discipline.

Scapegoat

Because principals are literally in charge of everything, they are the first to blame when something goes wrong. They are scapegoated by the staff, the central office, parents, and the general community. At Albion, the arson that resulted in the reconstitution of the "8:00 rule" was viewed as the failure of the principal to protect the building. The responsibility for students hanging out in the parking lot or cruising in their cars when they are supposed to be in school is laid at the feet of the building administration. Parent complaints about teachers mean the principal cannot maintain a competent staff. Lack of funds to support a speech and debate team means the principal doesn't care about academic pursuits. Wherever principals turn, they are held responsible for the shortcomings of their buildings.

Initially, at least, the principal expects and wants the school ("his school") to bear the stamp of his conception of what good education and a school are—the principal wants to be and feel influential (Sarason, 1971).

Educational Leader

Every principal wants to be an educational leader. Few get the chance. Preeminently, there is the time factor. As our narrative of life at Albion High School shows, and as our description of the multiple roles of the principal supports, there is not much time built into the structure of the position for meaningful educational dialogue, planning, and evaluation. And the formal time that is scheduled is often misdirected. Witness the elaborate teacher evaluation process mandated at Albion from the superintendent's office: pre-conference, observations with documentation, post-conference. What actually transpires is cursory and uninteresting. It certainly has little to do with educational leadership. What opportunity that exists for real leadership is marked by serendipity and opportunism, by seizing the moment as it is presented.

When complimenting a teacher for a well-constructed and well-taught lesson, an administrator is making a statement that excellence is recognized and rewarded. When meeting with a teacher whose classroom is in revolt, the principal is expressing concern about what happens behind the closed doors of a classroom and signals a change from previous administrators who have given high marks to a teacher needing improvement. When attending department meetings that focus on curricular issues, the principal is supporting dialogue and informed action. All of these events and actions may be defined as educational leadership—not rational, linear, and planned; but ad hoc, responsive, and realistic. Educational leadership happens, when it happens at all, within the cracks and around the edges of the job as defined and presently constituted.

Moral Authority

Finally, principals are the chief moral authority in a school. It is their notion of justice that prevails. Principals can maintain neutrality and let things progress as they always have; even that is a moral statement. Or they may take an active stance, threatening the assumptions of staff members and moving a school in more progressive or more regressive directions. Principals condone or condemn certain behaviors and attitudes; they model moral precepts as they go about the job. When the administrators at Albion took the side of minority students in the lunchroom radio incident, they gave a clear message to faculty that discrimination by race was not to be tolerated. A powerful message was transmitted. Had there been administrative apathy, an equally powerful point would have been made. At root, principals' actions are statements about justice. The role of moral authority is one that principals can seize and make their own; or it is one, like educational leadership, they can avoid and leave the mantle unclaimed.

To be sure, no two principals have the same job, but most experience common conditions, problems, tasks, worries. Each confronts the same constellation of parents, students, teachers, buildings, school board members, legal decisions, budget decisions, curriculum decisions, and the central office . . . Principals are dealt a hand of cards to play as best they can; the rules are that the cards may be shuffled, but neither discarded or added to (Barth, 1981).

We have sought to present both a description and analysis of the role of the principal. Although in many ways our narrative of a "week in the life of . . ." may be viewed as atypical, in more ways it is typical; it speaks to the difficulties of being an effective leader in a world where interactive issues and management concerns take center stage. It graphically illustrates the tensions, frustrations, dissatisfactions of the job along with its challenges, promises, and rewards.

In our efforts to cluster and codify the multiplicity of roles that comprise a principalship, we have sought to unravel some of the complexity and uncertainty, ambiguity, and contradiction endemic to the job. The role of the principal is not easy to understand; it is more difficult yet to fulfill.

Implications: There is No Magic

The principal is the gatekeeper of change. If you had to pick one figure in the school system who really matters in terms of whether you get change or not, it is the principal (Berman and McLaughlin, 1978).

There is much written of late about the power of the principal to make change and school improvements happen. It is almost as if there is a magic in the office that, when touched, transforms a mediocre school into an outstanding one, turns an apathetic faculty into enthusiastic professionals, and merges conflicting individual wants and needs into collective goals. A good principal, the story goes, can create a school where children learn and teachers develop, and where openness, cooperation, and harmony reign supreme. We want to challenge that notion a bit because, given what we know about the role, such a view of the principal seems in conflict with much of reality.

The World of "Is" and the World of "Ought"

The reality is that there is a huge gap between what the role of the principal is supposed to be and what is actually done in practice. For principals there are two worlds: the world of "is," how things actually are; and the world of "ought," how we would like things to be.

- Principals ought to be leaders; more likely they are managers.
- Principals ought to be helpers and developers; more often they are evaluators and judges.
- Principals ought to share knowledge; they are more characteristically keepers of secrets.
- Principals ought to be democratic; circumstances dictate that they are more autocratic in some decisions.
- Principals ought to show concern for individual problems and individual growth; but they are in charge of the whole school and often have to sacrifice personal vision for a more general view.
- Principals ought to be long-range in thinking; they are more often short-range. They are required to make instantaneous responses that keep small brush fires from becoming major conflagrations.
- Principals ought to be colleagues; they are bosses.
- Principals ought to be innovators; they are maintainers of the status quo.
- Principals ought to be champions of ideas; they are masters of the concrete. Attention to detail comes before concern for abstractions.

These are but a few of the contradictions between what principals hear they ought to be and know they are.

Ultimately, principals must make choices about how they will be and what they will become. They have at least three clear options.

1. They can choose to live totally within the world of is and in so doing disparage the world of ought. In this instance, principals opt to be good managers and not good leaders; they support and maintain the status quo and resist attempts to change things. They may become oppressive or become laissez-faire. In either case, they neither initiate nor actively support school improvements.

2. They can choose to live tentatively in the world of is, with one eye cocked toward the world of ought. By so doing, they leave themselves open to outside influences to take a step toward leadership, toward questioning the status quo, and toward school improvements. They may not initiate improvement activities, but they can be won over. They can lend the support of the principal's office to the programs and plans of others.

3. They can take the leap. They can take on the behaviors that effective leadership requires. They can become helpers, more democratic and open, more involved in individual growth issues, more long-range, more collegial, more innovative, and more involved in the world of ideas.

Principals who take this third option are capable of both initiating improvements and supporting the efforts of others.

There is NO Magic

If there were magic in the world, we would have all principals choose the third option. Having done that, we would then innoculate each of them with a formula that guarantees effective leadership and assures improvement and change in schools. But there is no magic; and there is no formula. The assistant principal at Albion High can attest to that. There are instead systematic and ad hoc attempts to make a dent in what is, to have an influence on what may become. These attempts take many forms. There is trial and error; there is persistence. There is a feeling for soft spots in the tough veneer of a school, identification of allies, seizing of opportunities within existing arrangements, mobilization of forces, garnering of resources, recognitions of excellence, offers to help, offers to listen. There is the bringing together of like people with like concerns, opening dialogue, questioning silences. There is the very act of being present, being attentive, and being ready.

And what of principals who can't or won't take these kinds of steps? Are we to assume there will be no change, no improvements because of them? We think not. Principals, like everyone else, are capable of change and growth and redirection. They welcome nurturance, attention, instruction, support, and rewards. If most principals are ill-prepared for their roles when they begin principaling, they are even less equipped to assume leadership once they have learned to get by as good managers. There has to be room made, space provided, and time devoted to the sustenance and development of principals. For those of us who work outside of schools to help improve them, there is an important role we can play in such an enterprise.

Finally, we want to express a point of view that goes against the current wisdom. Principals are important; they may even be critical. But they are not the only initiators and supporters of change. They are not our last and only hope. Leadership is interactive. A school shapes a principal as much as a principal shapes a school. A teacher or a group of teachers with an idea may influence a principal without ideas. A school in need of leadership may find it somewhere other than in the principal's office. Making improvements does not depend on one person, one variable, one idea. For we have learned from our experience that even with the best of leaders in the most ideal of conditions, nothing is assured.

There is no magic, for teachers and principals live with a set of unavoidable conflicts and tensions. It is the way they get worked out on a daily basis that differentiates one school from another.

Teachers want the principal to set up the condition that will make it possible for them to teach. They want a principal who is fair . . . not too many rules . . . warm, helpful and accessible. Under these conditions they will accept the principal's authority even as they bend it, shape it and influence it (Lortie, 1983).

References

Barth, Roland. "A Principal and His School." *The National Elementary Principal* 56 (Nov./Dec. 1976): 9–21.

Barth, Roland. *Run School Run.* Cambridge: Harvard University Press, 1980.

Barth, Roland. "A Principal's Center." *Journal of Staff Development* 2, 1 (May 1981): 52–69.

Berman, Paul, and McLaughlin, Milbrey. "Federal Programs Supporting Educational Change." Santa Monica: The Rand Corporation, 1978.

Berlingame, Martin. "Some Neglected Dimensions in the Study of Educational Administration." *Educational Administration Quarterly* 15, 1 (Winter 1979): 1–18.

Berlingame, Martin. "Staff Development for School Administrators: An Anthropological Approach." *Journal of Staff Development* 2, 1 (May 1981): 6–12.

Gross, Neal, and Herriott, Robert. *Staff Leadership in Public Schools.* New York: John Wiley and Sons, 1965.

Lortie, Dan. "School Teachers and Their Principals." Speech before the Metropolitan School Study Council at Wave Hill, Riverdale, New York, November 1983.

Sarason, Seymour. *The Culture of the School and the Problems of Change.* Boston: Allyn and Bacon, 1971.

Waller, Willard. *The Sociology of Teaching.* New York: John Wiley and Sons, 1932.

Wolcott, Henry F. *The Man in the Principal's Office, An Ethnography.* New York: Holt, Rinehart & Winston, 1973.

5

Studies of School Improvement Efforts: Some Necessary Understandings

In the social arena one is always dealing with competing statements of a problem and there is no time or attention to experiment in implementation with one or another of the formulations: that the choice of formulations has less to do with data than with the traditions, values, world outlooks, and the spirit of the times.

—Seymour Sarason, 1971

In the previous chapters, we concentrated on the lives of teachers and the realities of working in schools. We began with teachers because we believe it is with teachers that school improvements begin, not with the specific idea, curriculum, organizational or structural change as many "experts" would have us believe.

Most of the literature on school change comes from a policy perspective or from a managerial perspective. One gets the view that teachers can be infinitely manipulated like puppets on a string. We want to build a strong case for looking at the world with a teacher's perspective. We ask questions such as: What is their work life like? What do improvement efforts mean to them? Are these efforts realistic given the complexity of most classrooms? What would enable teachers to enhance their repertoire? What are the barriers to effective improvement? What strategies consider the complexity of the teacher's work? When do we use research, case materials, intuition, experience? How can we put all of this together in some way that meaningfully informs the people working in school improvement efforts?

When we write about teachers, we take as a given that most teachers learn their roles through experience—that style emerges from work in a specific context over time. This style develops in response to major dilemmas. For the elementary teacher there are issues of:

- More subjects to teach than time to teach them
- Coverage vs. mastery
- Large-group vs. small-group instruction
- When to stay with a subject or a routine and when to shift
- How to discipline students without destroying the class
- How to deal with isolation from other adults.

For secondary teachers dilemmas are rooted in the complexity of the formal and informal system, such as:

- Personal vs. organization constraints
- Dealing with the classroom and with the whole school
- Packaging and pacing instruction to fit into allocated time periods
- Proportioning subject matter expertise and affective needs in some way
- Figuring out how to deal with mixed loyalties to the faculty and to the student culture.

For both elementary and secondary teachers, there are the shared issues of being part of a profession where teaching and learning links are uncertain, where the knowledge base is weak, and where isolation is the norm. These understandings about teaching provide a starting point for developing understandings about schools and about the prospects for improving them.

In this chapter, we begin with a set of studies that take as their major concern the culture of schools and the process of school improvement. Some focus on the whole school, some on individual teachers, some on conflicts between insiders and outsiders who work with each other. In reviewing these studies, we get more focused descriptions of the teacher and we begin to get a feel for many of the barriers to school improvement; not the least of these is understanding the full array of forces involved in school improvement. These descriptions raise some new questions and new problems for us.

> We thought naively, that with appropriate incentives and enablers, across a variety of organizational settings, and for any and all innovations, the same kinds of people would do the proposing, and the same kinds of others, the adopting. Neat, simple, precise, and predictable—but wrong (Daft and Becker, 1978).

But we are getting ahead of ourselves. This chapter pulls together a number of school improvement efforts of the last decade.[1] When taken as a group, they begin to repeat certain themes. We discuss these themes and some understandings that we need for our work in schools. These understandings are broadened and deepened by others who have reviewed, studied, observed, and experienced schools as complex institutions. Working in this way, we begin to build some tools that we need—some conceptual tools—so that we may repeat our successes and avoid mistakes that we and others have already made.

The School Culture

Perhaps the most compelling theme, yet the one least understood, is the penetrating description of schools as cultures. From Sarason's (1971) earliest description of the "behavioral" and "programmatic" regularities of elementary schools, which illuminated for the first time the unrelenting routine of the teacher's life, to Smith and Keith's (1971) day-by-day description of the attempt to try to build an innovative school, this theme appears and reappears. We begin to understand not only the complicated work of the teacher (putting together the subject matter and organizing it), but all the other links that somehow make a school: the leadership, the interpersonal relations among the people, the individual personalities, the context of the school, and those ideas that look great on paper but often can't be transformed and made workable. (See Figure 1, at pages 96–99.)

Sussman's (1977) "Tales" alert us to the behind-the-scenes interplay between principals' and teachers' tensions that exist when the leadership cares more about its own future than about communicating with the people who would do the work. She also shows us how strong the

---

[1]We admit to being selective of those studies and descriptions that reveal what can be learned about teachers, their work, and what happens as teachers and principals attempt to improve practices in schools.

teacher culture can be when teachers decide they are behind a change and have had a role in shaping it. What we learn about the culture is that real changes in practice involve time, often additional personnel, some type of expertise, and usually some additional materials.

Grace's (1978) work calls attention to elementary teachers' tremendous desire for "being good." He documents how this attitude stands in the way of teachers' ability to look at their own practices. We learn also that much of the vulnerability and protectiveness is built into systems where ideas do not flow freely, but are locked into each classroom. We suspect that these attitudes grow because much of the teacher's learning is picked up along the way and codified, not in any public way, but privately stored by each teacher (Gibson, 1973). It is easy to see where these attitudes can create a wary and suspicious culture.

There's a Teacher's Center nearby but I suppose it's ingrained in us to feel heels to ask for time off to go there. You know quite well that it means your colleague is going to be ditched with fifty or sixty or more children while you're away, and for that morning the children are going to suffer (Gibson, 1973, p. 246).

In an attempt to understand six months' worth of observing open education in England, the Berlaks (1981) describe 16 dilemmas inherent in their preferences and descriptions of schooling. They group these dilemmas under a *control* set, a *curriculum* set, and *a societal* set, which are then used in conjunction with descriptions of teachers' classrooms. Using these dilemmas as a language of inquiry, we focus again on the range of "tensions 'in' teachers, 'in' the situation, and 'in' society, over the nature of control teachers exert over children in school."

Goodlad's (1984) long-term study is the most recent and contemporary description of the complexity of both the differences and similarities of schools. They seem to look the same. Teachers stand in front of the class. Students take tests, answer questions, do seat work. Instructional practices are similar. Grouping arrangements are easily identified from school to school. But schools differ even as schooling appears similar. The differences show up in things outside the pedagogical sphere. Interaction between students and teachers is different. The academic orientation differs from school to school. Peer groups are strong in all schools, but their influence and their interests are not the same. Principals and teachers respect one another in some places while they view each other as strangers in others. These views of the differences among schools should make us cautious about oversimplifying our descriptions of schools and attempts at applying universal solutions. We see this more clearly as we look at attempts to rationalize school processes in the following studies.

Linear Paths vs. Detours

We come to learn that innovations of all kinds fail to consider the huge amounts of time involved in implementing new procedures while continuing daily to keep the class going. Wolcott's (1977) case study dramatically illustrates the imposition of a rational/linear scheme on a district where the clash between technology and the teacher's reality caused conflict and the eventual demise of the project (the attempted implementation of Program Planning Budgeting Systems). Here we see the clash of the values of technology—values of prediction control and clarity—with the teacher's values of autonomy, experiential learning, and ad-hocism. And, again, Charter's (1973) case study illustrates the incredible energy investment and costs of implementing differentiated staffing. His documentation reveals the inordinate amount of time that made this structural innovation far more costly than rewarding and hence unusable.

Daft and Becker's (1978) multiyear study of 13 high school districts provides a classic case of expecting organizational changes to run smoothly and in a straight line. What is actually observed are the more salient features of innovative schools, which turn out to be the number and type of support staff available, as well as the degree of teacher professionalism. The authors coin the phrase "idea champions," and call attention to the fact that it is teachers themselves, who, when highly professional, are the real innovators who learn about ideas and how to use them.

Two additional in-depth case studies begin to show more clearly the great variety in schools as well as the circuitous paths taken by individual schools in their efforts to implement innovative ideas. Huberman and Miles (1982), investigating 12 schools in ten states, found that they could array the schools in terms of their *supporting conditions* (core vs. peripheral application, operates on a regular daily basis, provides payoffs to users, and receives administrative support); *passage completion* (goes from soft to hard money, job description becomes standard, skills are included in formal training routines established); and *cycle survival* (survives annual budget cycles, survives departure of new personnel, achieves widespread use throughout school, and survives equipment turnover). Popkowitz and others (1982) take one innovation—Individually Guided Education (IGE)—and document its effects by looking at three dimensions of schooling: work, knowledge, and professionalism. They describe the different normative climates of the schools they study and the teachers' different understandings of curriculum, instruction, and evaluation.

Isolation and Insulation

We learn that the role of teacher lends itself to private struggles of both great heroism and great cowardice as teachers unlock and facilitate important learnings for students but then won't talk to teachers on the lower floors because conventional wisdom says that 6th grade teachers know more than 1st grade teachers (McPherson, 1972). Sometimes the insulation of the classroom is so strong that teachers forget they have their students for only a small portion of the day. Parents, who are uninformed and whose expectations are ignored, can often be formidable opponents to innovation (Barth, 1972).

We come to understand that school improvements involve a complex array of understandings—not just of the ideas, mandates, or new thrust of the superintendent, but of the people who inhabit schools and the complicated functions in the building.

Do Unto Others . . .

Over more than a decade of school improvement efforts have taught us that there are some necessary conditions for change. But they are difficult to describe since they lend themselves to what appears to be the obvious; nonetheless, they keep reappearing. For example, in the four volumes of the League of Cooperating Schools and the Rand Change Agent Study (Berman and McLaughlin, 1978),[2] we find the following conditions for change:

- The importance of early participation in thinking and planning school improvement efforts
- Concrete practical classroom activities
- A process labeled Dialog, Decisionmaking, and Action
- Meetings focus on particular activities for improvement
- Teachers can support each other when they are publicly supported by the principal

---

[2]The League of Cooperating Schools' research group worked for five years studying the process of change. The Rand Study visited 293 sites and made in-depth studies of 25 schools.

- Teacher expertise can be encouraged through visitations and sharing—but it doesn't just happen; it takes time and much encouragement
- Projects are easier to begin when participants volunteer. Volunteers help because they want to and are open to commiting themselves to innovation.

Gibson (1973) and Sussman (1977) also note from their observation and interviews with teachers that when teachers are given time for reflection, experimentation, and choice, they engage in studying and enhancing their practices. In short, the obvious strikes us once again: when we treat teachers as we would have them treat students, they respond more readily with openness, engagement, and commitment. When we facilitate for others, we should take care to provide rather than tell, teach rather than preach, and acknowledge complexity rather than rush to simplify.

Between Two Worlds There is a Chasm!

Still other school improvement studies alert us to the enormous gap between those who study schools and those who do the work of schools (Emrick and Peterson, 1978; Gross, Giacquinta, and Bernstein, 1971; Smith and Keith, 1971).

Two in-depth studies (Gross and others, and Smith and Keith) look at innovation in a single school. In the former, the teachers are asked to change their role from teller to "catalytic agent." The researchers struggle to find out what it means to be a catalyst, as the teachers struggle to find out how to do it. The researchers test the theory of resistance to change, while the teachers attempt to get help and support from their administrator. The case study ends with a focus on implementation and adds to our understanding of the necessary components of implementation from the teacher's perspective. They are:
- A clear description of the innovation
- Teacher training
- Commitment to the ideal
- Materials
- Organizational arrangements to aid implementation.

The lack of understanding of how to translate new roles into personal/social and organizational realities is abundantly clear in this case. In the latter, Smith and Keith attempt to understand innovation in schools by studying teaching, learning, and administering a school. The authors document the first year of the creation of a new school and conceptualize for the reader the gulf between what innovators imagine and the way schools actually work. We begin to understand a new set of dilemmas when we think about and attempt to make significant changes in schools. Questions and some possible answers emerge, revealing the tangled web of human relations, ideal and real conditions, and the problem of newness.

- How does one translate "the mandate" into daily life without losing the essence?
- Who should be hired for an innovative setting (new, inexperienced teachers who are untarnished by tradition or experienced teachers more set in their ways)?
- What should go on in planning time? (Part of school jargon is planning and even preplanning. There was money and time in this case. What do you work on—values, skills, organization?)
- What should the role of leadership be?
- There were big ideas like "continuous progress" and "non-gradedness." How do they get translated into curriculum? To school organization? To what teachers do in the classroom?

Both these studies and others like them help us understand once again that:

1. Students come every day.
2. The curriculum needs to be organized.
3. Teachers need to have a repertoire of knowledge, skills, and abilities to handle different modes of organizing.
4. Groups of students must be managed.
5. The more teachers are involved with each other, the more time, energy, and skills are needed.
6. There will never be enough resources.
7. The human organization of schools is complicated by many conflicting values over what schools are for, different personalities, differences in abilities, and the constraints and possibilities of different contexts.

If we put these studies together with others that have tried to sort out the maze of complexity of schools and try to cull what we know, we begin to get a set of understandings about schools as organizations, about teachers, and about the process of school improvement. These understandings form the foundation and conceptual background of our knowledge. (See Figures 2, 3, 4, at pages 100–103.)

Schools Are Not The Same—Differences Make a Difference

Schools are not all the same, nor are classrooms. We have a growing body of knowledge that describes certain conditions of schools that affect the possibilities for school improvement. School people have always said that you can "feel" the climate of a school when you walk into the main office. Studies such as Reutter's (1979), Bentzen's (1974), and Goodlad's (1984) begin to give us some conceptual tools that back up the folk wisdom. Local conditions differ in many significant ways. These have been well documented by Miles (1967) and others. These conditions, when understood, form the dynamic that help us understand the school as a complex organization. When a school has vital leadership, committed staff, and support from the community, it is ready to make improvements. But when leadership is fearful or sees its role as keeping the status quo, much of the climate shifts and teachers spend much time protecting themselves and keeping to themselves. School improvement activities also depend on the capacity of schools to initiate and sustain improvements or innovations. Whether a school needs to be encouraged to change or given help depends on the local conditions.

The most extensive current discussion of the differences among schools is described as the "effective schools research." It has been so named because schools having certain characteristics have been described as effective and compared with others seen as less effective (Reutter, 1979; Edmonds, 1978; Austin, 1979; Squires, 1980; Brookover and Lezotte, 1979). The characteristics of effective schools, as defined by these researchers, are:

- A sense of order in the school
- High staff expectations for student achievement
- Strong leadership from the principal or other staff members
- Schoolwide control of instructional and training decisions
- Clear goals collectively agreed upon.

This line of research has an intuitive logic that has made it very popular among school people. The characteristics are important as descriptors of what effective schools look like, but not as recipes for effectiveness. They overlook and underplay the significance of individual variation among schools and often hide the difficulty of achieving these purposes. The hard work is still to be done in finding strategies that make schools work.

Most successful school change efforts will be messier and more idiosyncratic than systematic and will need to focus on collaborative, whole school reform (Purkey and Smith, 1982).

While some schools may do well to model their structure for school improvement on the effective schools research, others may find this approach totally inappropriate. We still need to struggle with appropriate strategies for each school district, strategies that attend sensitively to local conditions.

We have talked about the culture of schools in our previous chapters. Anyone who has ever worked in an organization has a sense of what is affirmed and what is scorned. These norms and values in a building are critical for understanding the expectations of the insiders and hence important for those who would make changes.

Teachers do not live and work in a vacuum. Although they may work in isolation, they are part of a larger context, and it is this connection that is hard to understand from the outside and often not considered from the inside.

The major error in dealing with problems of organizational change, both at the practical and theoretical level is to disregard the systemic properties of the organization and to confuse individual change with modifications in organizational variables.

In short, to approach institutional change solely in individual terms involves an impressive and discouraging set of assumptions . . .

The behavior of people in organizations is still the behavior of individuals but it has a different set of determinants than behavior outside organizational roles (Katz and Kahn, 1966).

Appearance vs. Reality

Instead of seeing school as an orderly, easily controlled organization, we are coming to understand that teachers and classes and schools may have very tenuous links to one another. What people talk about is hampered by an uncodified set of practices that are learned often in isolation. (This may, in part, be why schools are having some success with various basic skills curricula. They provide a language that can be shared by principal and teachers.)

The craft of teaching has been skillfully described by several people (Lortie, 1975; Waller, 1967; Jackson, 1968; Dreeben, 1970). These understandings raise once again the reality of what teachers' work life looks like from their perspective. Rather than framing a teacher's work by discussions of goals and objectives, we see dilemmas, tensions, and choices. When we add our understandings of the school as an organization, we begin to see that learning one's teacher role in an isolated fashion, while living daily in a presumably collective environment, may be the ultimate paradox for school improvers. What we come to understand is that school improvement strategies are usually based on the appearance of collectivity rather than the reality of isolation. We need to know how to work with teachers who have been isolated from one another, how to provide experiences in collective activities, as well as in individual enterprises that are mutually supportive. This, like many of our understandings, is easier said than done.

Stages of Change

Recently, school improvers have begun to document phases or stages in school improvement processes (Berman and McLaughlin, 1978; Emrick and Peterson, 1978). The earliest descriptions were made in 1947 when Kurt Lewin talked about the stages of change during his many studies on group interaction. At that time, he drew attention to the fact that there appear to be three stages of change as groups are introduced to new ways of behaving. The stages were unfreezing, changing, and refreezing.

Lewin's descriptions speak to an initial period (unfreezing) where people are threatened by new ideas or confronted with different ways of looking at what they do. This is a period of great discomfort, where much support is necessary to help people receive new ideas. The second stage (changing) is characterized by participating in new ways of doing things. The third stage attempts to lock the ideas into one's repertoire. The stages are not discrete; it is often difficult to see where one stage ends and another begins. These descriptors are useful, however, in alerting us to ways of thinking and understanding how people grow and change. Several authors have given these stages different names, but the essentials are similar.

Before we become too comfortable with stage theories, we should remember that people don't automatically move from one stage to the other. Some people get stuck; others race by us; and still others wait to be facilitated. Much gets unleashed during each phase. Meetings and information that may be very rewarding and interesting in the initial stages are often seen as time consuming, even irrelevant, as teachers begin to experiment in their own classrooms.

The Political Nature of Changes

Strong value positions may be embedded in innovations that come to districts and schools. Innovations are often sold based on assumptions of what is good for students or society. Besides presenting the problem of translating innovations into practical means for the teacher, particular innovations become highly politicized (House, 1974; Corwin, 1973) and educational concerns recede. Changes that disrupt business as usual often have strong moral components and commitments; as people organize to make changes, politics, power, and pressure groups take on a life of their own unrelated to the innovation (see Gold and Miles, 1981).

Participation—Who? When? How?

Some researchers balk at the fact that the definitions of participation in innovative activity have not been clear (Giacquinta, 1973). Those of us who have experienced involvement in improvement projects are well aware of the thorny problems of involving people in the change process. Mandating everyone to be involved may work *if* the leadership is sensitive and supportive and rewards are hard to refuse. Yet forcing people to do things against their will can bring resistance, hostility, and negative responses. On the other hand, asking for volunteers provides an initially committed group, but raises the question of how others are to become involved. Volunteers may not need what is being offered. When to involve people is also not well understood. Our firmly held values about participation can become oppressive, especially as meetings become a way of life. In many schools, the growth of a star system can be more disruptive than helpful.

Again, we want to call attention to the subtleties of the school culture and the importance of dealing with participation as a necessary, important, potentially problematic, and powerful process of school improvement. More study will only be useful if we pay attention to the different contingencies under which different modes of participation take place and are effective.

Top-Down, Bottom-Up: Not Either-Or, But Both

Much of the recent past literature in education has been dominated by managerial perspectives. The assumption has been that people on the top can dictate what the people on the bottom will do. But there is much turmoil in the managerial field today (Griffiths, 1979; Clark, 1981). Historical alliances have changed. Teachers have organized. An upward drift of policy has put much of the social change policies in the hands of the federal bureaucracy and state legislatures. We have a relatively new phenomenon for educational policy, which has previously been dominated by superintendents.

Any discussion of authority must consider how people are involved in activities, how they are supported, how interactions take place, and how innovative and supportive norms are built. Posing the problem as strictly managerial puts the focus only on leadership. But likewise looking only at home-grown improvements puts the focus only on teachers. Both policy from the top and engagement from the bottom deal with the process of improvement. One without the other leaves out a significant part of the process.

Implementation—or What Happens in the Classroom

What actually happens in the classroom as a result of a new mandate, new reading program, new management system, new thrust by the district on law related activities? This question has become a critical one as we move from counting how many new programs are being initiated to finding out what actually happens when teachers go back to their classrooms. We now know that teachers must have practical activities that fit their classroom reality or be shown through actual demonstrations how they can be changed. Furthermore, implementation must be accompanied by personalized support, often in-class help, time to learn information on a variety of levels, mobilization of a supportive staff, and leadership that is sensitive to the kinds of resources and organizational arrangements necessary to make implementing new curricular, organizational, or instructional ideas work (Cox, 1983).

Pulling It All Together: Schools, Teachers, and School Improvement

If we pull together our understandings about schools, teachers, and the process of change, we can shed some light on the extreme complexity of making improvements. We can begin to better understand the school—the institution everyone knows, but doesn't really know.

The school is an organization peopled by those who have learned their roles by experiencing them. Each school has a unique culture just like the thousands of offices and factories in the country, only the institution is public and charged with teaching children. As the culture moves and shifts, new ideas are advanced and the school is supposed to accommodate these ideas. Outsiders are in a hurry to see schools adopt new ideas, but the time perspective of the insiders is different.

The area where there is pressure to change is the area we know the least about: the teacher and instruction. We can describe schools, principals, teachers, and students. And we can create materials of all kinds. But when we struggle to understand the culture, its people, and its substance, we must acknowledge that each school is different, that the collection of people and their history together form different ways of being. Teachers deal with a series of dilemmas worked out daily in their classrooms. Their salient culture is their own classroom. Ideas for improvements come to the school and then a host of other factors are unleashed.

In effect, schools are like families where unspoken understandings dominate. There are characters, strong personalities, leaders, those to be tolerated. There are ways of being open or being closed. There are people who are listened to and people who are ignored. As in the family in all its complexity, there are those endless tensions that one learns to tolerate. In school, there are the dilemmas of teaching, managing between one's own class and the school culture, and handling the effects of leadership on one's own sense of self. There are the endless shibboleths about doing it all for the children while ignoring the adults and the interaction between them.

The teacher learns in much the same way a child learns, through active manipulation and participation in the environment (Field, 1979).

Participation, continued support, rewards and resources, and the excitement of becoming more competent are all part of the needed conditions for improvement. But, like families, different people need different things at different times. Sometimes what is rewarding at one time turns out to be draining at another; what one person needs experience in may have always been part of the repertoire of another. The family feeling persists in spite of these differences. Teachers go back to their own classrooms after an inservice day as family members go back to work after a vacation, filled with exhilaration, frustration; old nagging realities and some fresh ideas become the new reality. Innovative ideas and mandates are similar to parental attempts to "tell" children what to do. Where there is possibility for involvement, experience, and participation, growth is possible. Where ideas cannot be translated into practical realities, there are lectures better left undelivered.

We have reviewed several decades of experience and research that enhance our understanding about school improvements and the different strategies and their uses. Description may not lead us to the skills we need to act; but description may help us understand the social realities of school improvement. With these understandings, we can continue to build a way to improve schools. We need to attend to how teachers actually work, how they come to learn their work, how schools function as complex social organizations, and how the process of change takes form.

Figure 1. Descriptions of School Improvement Efforts

Source	Major Focus	Some Conclusions
The Culture of the School and the Problem of Change (Sarason, 1971).	A description of the attempt to implement modern math into elementary school.	Schools are cultures of their own. In order to make any real changes, one must understand the behavioral and programmatic regularities of teachers and the importance of the role of the principal.
Implementing Organizational Innovations (Gross, Giacquinta, and Bernstein, 1971).	A case study of an attempt to change the teacher's role from teller to catalyst or facilitator.	The innovation must be clear to the staff. Experiences must be provided to learn. Some measure of willingness or commitment is necessary. Materials and/or equipment must be available. Organizational arrangement compatible with the innovation must be made.
Open Education and the American School (Barth, 1972).	Chapter three describes the "Romance and Reality" of trying to implement a new ideology into an elementary school (open education).	The chapter calls attention to the complexity of all those concerned with making major changes in school: administrators, teachers, and the community. Care must be taken to understand not only the rhetoric of innovation, but the values of all the groups and a great possibility that there will be conflict.
The study of the League of Cooperating Schools: *The Power to Change: Issues for the Innovative Educator* (Culver and Hoban, 1973); *Changing Schools: The Magic Feather Principle* (Bentzen, 1974); *Effecting Organizational Renewal in Schools* (Williams and others, 1974); *The Dynamics of Educational Change* (Goodlad, 1975).	All four of these books come from a five-year study of a group of 18 schools joined together to create a league. The focus of the study was to better understand the conditions necessary for schools to solve their own problems with a group supportive of this new norm.	Efforts at school improvement involve new knowledge but also provisions for continuous support. A process described as *Dialog, Decisionmaking, and Action* (DDA) traces what goes on between faculty and principal during improvement efforts. Over time, teachers can be convinced that much of the expertise can be legitimated and found among innovative teachers themselves.
Anatomy of Educational Innovation (Smith and Keith, 1971).	The day-by-day description of the creation of a unique school with the latest in modern architecture, curriculum, school organization, and innovative leadership. The book describes the first year.	Some key understandings about unanticipated consequences, the gap between ideals and realities of schools, problems of leadership, and some greater understanding of strategies of grandeur and gradualism are explained.

Teachers vs. Technocrats (Wolcott, 1977).	The study of the attempted implementation of PPBS in a school district and its subsequent demise. An ethnographic description is used.	There are indeed different realities. The teacher reality involves the need for autonomy, the value that only teachers know teaching; there is ambivalence about change and strong feelings of vulnerability by teachers. For technocrats, the key themes are rationality, prediction, management, and clarity. For teachers, key themes are autonomy, experience, and adhocism.
Tales Out of School: Implementing Organizational Change in the Elementary Grades (Sussman, 1977).	The study of three schools implementing organizational innovations (individualized instruction and two open classrooms).	Many innovations are going on besides those made public. Resources to aid in implementation include expertise, personnel, time, and materials. Many innovations are "underdeveloped." Organizational innovations often create additional conflicts in goals, teachers' traditional rewards, and conflicts with administrators.
Measuring the Implementation of Differentiated Staffing (Charter, 1973).	The comparison of two schools: one making a full-scale effort at implementing a major innovation, and another where there was no implementation. The instruments used build on case study data.	The comparison reveals the hidden costs of time involved in innovation—time taken away from normal teaching demands (disruption effects). Structural changes may have little or no effect.
Fifteen Thousand Hours: Secondary Schools and Their Effects on Children (Reutter and others, 1979).	A three-year study of 12 secondary schools in Britain. The focus was on different influences on students due to differences in the social organization of the schools.	All of the schools had a similar student population. They differed not in physical, administrative, or organizational factors, but in their characteristics as social institutions: degree of academic emphasis, availability of incentives and rewards, teacher actions in lessons. All of these factors were open to modification by the staff.
The Innovative Organization (Daft and Becker, 1978).	A multiyear study of the many variables related to organizational innovativeness, such as support staff, organizational complexity, teacher professionalism. The study took place in 13 high school districts.	The authors admit to the complexity of organizational change and revise their theory in order to better explain their findings. They draw distinctions between administrative innovations and teacher innovations. "Idea champions" seem to enhance innovativeness.
Teacher, Ideology, and Control: A Study in Urban Education (Grace, 1978).	The purpose of this study was to examine, in both historical and sociological terms, the teachers of the	Despite the autonomy of urban teachers, the constraints of the work and "being good" have precluded teachers from challenge and critical reflection about their own activities. "The

Figure 1. Descriptions of School Improvement Efforts (continued)

Source	Major Focus	Some Conclusions
	urban working class. The study takes place in London in ten comprehensive schools with 105 teachers from 1975 to 1977.	irony is that people who are engaged in explaining the world are precluded from doing this in their own situation. . . ."
Small Town Teacher (McPherson, 1972).	A year-long participant observation study of a rural elementary school. The author was one of the teachers. Her attempt was to describe the social system of a rural school day and the interactions, norms, and sanctions of the system.	Teachers display very defensive attitudes toward their work. Norms are subtle, such as: good teachers can leave their doors open because they are in control of the class. There is little interaction between teachers of different grade levels; in fact, teachers on the lower floor who teach younger children are held in lower esteem than those on the upper floor.
Teachers Talking—Aims, Methods, Attitudes to Change (Gibson, 1973).	Two hundred and twelve teachers were interviewed in 46 schools to find out the different ways teachers see their work and the means they evolve to cope with change.	A penetrating analysis of interviews of teachers in elementary and secondary schools highlighting the way teachers learn to teach, the way their attitudes toward children are formed, and their need for direct experience in discovering other ways to handle teaching and learning. An example of this method is described to show how teachers' experiences can directly change how they motivate, control, and provide for a more collective classroom that involves mutual obligation rather than teacher domination.
Beyond Surface Curriculum: An Interview Study of Teachers' Understandings (Bussis, Chittenden, and Amarel, 1976).	The purpose of this study was to investigate the understandings and constructs that teachers use. Teachers were associated with an advisory program that sponsored an "open education" approach to instruction. Includes in-depth interviews of 60 teachers.	The study documents teachers' understandings about the child as resource, the teacher as investigator, the nature of adult relationships in the school, and more. The study uses practice to help build theory about teaching and learning. Provides readers with a comprehensive view of the teacher and the total environment within which the teacher works.
Federal Programs Supporting Educational Change, Volume III (Berman and McLaughlin, 1978).	The U.S. Office of Education sponsored a several-year study to look at federally funded programs designed to	A major contribution of the study was to turn the focus to the problem of implementation: how does the new idea actually get into the school? Effective strategies were (1) concrete;

Reference	Description	Findings
	introduce and spread innovative practices. A summary of the findings.	teacher-specific and extended training; (2) classroom assistance: from project or district staff; (3) teacher observation of similar projects elsewhere; (4) meetings that focused on practical problems; (5) teacher participation in project decisions; (6) local materials development; (7) principal participation in training.
A Synthesis of Findings Across Five Recent Studies in Educational Dissemination and Change (Emrick and Peterson, 1978).	Summarizes the findings of five major studies in educational change. Includes a cross-site analysis of the major issues and implications for people involved in school improvement projects.	Five major generalizations emanating from this analysis are: (1) Meaningful change occurs as a process, not as an event. (2) Directed *personal* intervention is the most potent form of support. (3) Continuous personal participation of the implementing staff is needed to firmly root and sustain utilization. (4) Administrators occupy a crucial role in supporting the utilization process. (5) Descriptive, instructional, and supportive materials are needed.
Innovation Up Close: A Field Study of 12 School Settings (Huberman and Miles, 1982).	These case studies were part of a larger study, the Study of Dissemination Efforts Supporting School Improvement, a nationwide examination of the effects of strategies developed with federal support.	The authors describe four different "families" of schools, characterized as *mandated stable use, skillful committed use, vulnerability,* and *indifference.* These different sets of conditions relate whether the innovations were expected to be institutionalized. The authors found that "Administrators push, demand, support, and think about the organization; teachers react, get involved, struggle with the demands of the innovation, and think about their lives with students."
The Myth of Educational Reform (Popkowitz, Tabachnick, and Wehlage, 1982).	A set of case studies of six schools that implemented Individually Guided Education. Authors show how the programs are accepted and changed in the six settings.	The authors describe three major adaptations to IGE: the *technical,* in which techniques become "the ends of school activity rather than the means"; the *constructivist,* which focuses on assumptions and definitions in which problem solving and integration are cornerstones of teachers' concepts of knowledge; and the *illusory,* in which activities and purposes seem unrelated.
Dilemmas of Schooling (Berlak and Berlak, 1981).	An in-depth study of open classrooms in England over a six-month period.	The authors create a language of dilemmas focusing on what they see as the central concerns of teaching and social change. These include dilemmas of *control* by the teacher, *curriculum* (how teachers transmit knowledge and ways of knowing and learning), and *societal* (differences in resource allocation, control of deviants, and the relationship of subgroups to dominant groups).

Figure 2. Understandings About Schools as Organizations

● Schools have certain properties that make work in them fraught with ambiguity. These properties form the backdrop of the teacher's work environment.
   a. Goals of schools are unclear.
   b. School people are vulnerable to the external environment.
   c. The work of schools is translated in many different ways. Teachers develop different teaching styles.
   d. How the work gets accomplished is generally not shared with the outside world.

(Bidwell, 1965; Clark and others, 1980; Dreeben, 1970; Lortie, 1975; McPherson, 1972; Miles, 1967; Sarason, 1971; Schlectz, 1976; Sieber, 1979; Waller, 1967; Wolcott, 1977.)

● The school "ethos" (the history, biography, social relations, and ideologies) within schools differ. These differences provide the hidden targets for school improvement efforts (that is, some schools have a history of innovative activity; some have always been traditional).

(Bentzen, 1974; Goodlad, 1975; Grace, 1978; Reutter, 1979.)

● Local school conditions have a great deal to do with how and if problems or possibilities for improvement take place. Local conditions include:
   Type of leadership: dynamic, oppressive, coping, surviving, maintaining
   Teaching staff: cosmopolitan, committed, routinized
   Community support: conflicted, supportive
   Resources: human and material
   Instructional ideology: one dimensional, multidimensional
   District ethos: unchanging, insensitive, supportive.

(Berman and McLaughlin, 1978; Elmore and McLaughlin, 1982; Goodlad, 1975; Reutter, 1979.)

● Principals affect the climate of the school and what gets rewarded. This role of variants of the role (team leadership) is critical to any improvement effort.
   The principal's role is more crucial in the elementary school where the setting is more family oriented and effects are felt more directly. In secondary schools, department chairs and assistant principals play more critical leadership roles.

(Barth, 1972; Bentzen, 1974; Burlingame, 1970; Emrick and Peterson, 1978; Lieberman, 1969; Lipham, 1977; Sarason, 1971; Sussman, 1977.)

● Schools are separate cultures of their own. One must understand what the norms and values are from the inside. These must be considered as part of any improvement strategy (for instance, who influences whom, who eats lunch together, how people interact).

(Maiocco, 1978; Sarason, 1971; Schlectz, 1976.)

● The time perspective of schools is misunderstood by more reformers. Much needless disappointment has to do with unrealistic demands upon school personnel. Their time perspective is the most critical, not that of the reformers.

(Burlingame, 1979; Charter, 1973; Gross, Giacquinta, and Bernstein, 1971; Sarason, 1971; Sussman, 1977; Wolcott, 1977.)

- Descriptions of school effectiveness or school successes give us conceptual understandings. For example, there are now several studies that describe the effective school. They have the following conditions:
  a. Strong leadership.
  b. More teacher time spent "on task."
  c. Good faculty communication on collective goals for the school.
  d. High expectations for students.
  e. Frequent student evaluations.
  f. Teacher focus on instruction.

(Austin, 1979; Brookover and Lezotte, 1979; Clark, Lotto, and McCarthy, 1980; Edmonds, 1978; Reutter, 1979; Squires, 1980.)

- School people generally agree on formal roles and on the general nature of why they are there. That is, there is a culture that the people understand. But in the area of instruction and teacher methods, there are few agreed upon policies or practices because of the complexity of teaching and the craft. Some refer to this as the weak technical culture of teaching. Organizationally, classrooms are loosely connected, and the schools in many districts are loosely joined to one another. Instruction is the least controlled activity. This is a key understanding of school improvement, for it is at the heart of most school improvement projects.

(Bidwell, 1965; Deal and Celotti, 1977; Feitler, 1980; Meyer, 1977; Meyer, Rowan, and Weick, 1976; Weick, 1976.)

- Innovations must be accommodated into an already existing mode of working. How ideas get adapted and changed is not well understood.

(Berman and McLaughlin, 1978; Crandall and others, 1982.)

Figure 3. Understandings About Teachers

● Most teachers learn their roles through experience. Their style is developed by their own struggle to deal with curriculum, students, and the expectations of their level of schooling. There is no one best teaching style for all students.
(Dreeben, 1970; Gibson, 1973; Grace, 1978; Lortie, 1975; McPherson, 1972; Waller, 1967.)

● Teachers are faced with major dilemmas. Elementary school teachers must deal with:
a. More subjects than there is time to teach them.
b. Coverage vs. mastery.
c. Large-group, small-group, and individualized instruction. When to shift is more art and craft than science.
d. Tremendous isolation from other adults.
(Kepler, 1980.)

● For secondary teachers, negotiating the complexity of the formal and informal system creates a different set of dilemmas. They are:
a. Personal control vs. organizational constraints. Secondary teachers need to deal with their own classrooms and the bureaucracy because rewards are tied to both organizational realities.
b. Fifty-minute periods and five or six different groups of students each day force a fast pace and a rhythm of its own that must be accommodated.
c. Adapting to being expert in subject matter causes focus on content, often at the expense of needed affective behavior.
d. Identification with the peer group vs. students causes mixed loyalties.

● Teaching, for the most part, is an isolated activity. That is, teachers work without adult interaction most of the day. Depending on a host of other factors (social context, history, school climate, leadership, and more), teachers are often involved in a very lonely job.

● High schools most closely resemble large-scale organizations. As such (and in spite of the fact that rules may be proposed at the principal level), the department is the social system most likely to affect the teacher.

● Teachers must be able to use innovations in a practical way. Their cry that ideas are "too theoretical" speaks often to the complexity of keeping the classroom operable while incorporating new ideas.

Figure 4. Understandings About the Process of School Improvement

● Effective school improvement requires attention to all relevant parts of the school: the school's norms, the rewards for work, necessary continuous support, needed structures, and necessary human and material resources.

(Baldridge and Deal, 1975; Fullan and Pomfret, 1982; Gross, Giacquinta, and Bernstein, 1971; Goodlad, 1975; Sieber, 1979.)

● There appear to be stages of change in the improvement process. They include: initiation (engagement, awareness), implementation (managing or changing), and incorporation (institutionalization). These stages, loosely defined, can aid in planning types of activities for improvement purposes.

(Berman, 1978; Giacquinta, 1973; Hall and Loucks, 1979; Lewin, 1947; McLaughlin, 1979; Zaltman, 1979.)

● Although there is some evidence that change occurs in stages, movement from one stage to another is not automatic. Furthermore, motivations, needs, conflicts, and rewards also change as stages change. What may be a reward at one stage may be seen as a punishment at another.

(Bentzen, 1974; Charter, 1973; Lieberman and Shiman, 1973; Sieber, 1979; Smith and Keith, 1971; Sussman, 1977.)

● Because of the lack of a precise technical culture and because ideas often come to a school or system via a particular person, ideas, innovations, or school improvements are often seen as political, or they may become political during the process of change. They move out of the educational arena into a political arena often accompanied by power plays, coalitions, and conflict.

(Barth, 1972; Gold and Miles, 1981; Gross, Giacquinta, and Bernstein, 1971; Smith and Keith, 1971; Sussman, 1977; Wolcott, 1977.)

● Although there is some disagreement as to the appropriate time teachers need to participate in school improvement (as initiators, primary decision makers, collaborators), there can be no question that continuous participation is a critical component in school improvement. Local conditions most probably dictate how many participants, which ones, at what stage, for how long, for what purpose, and in what capacity.

(Bentzen, 1974; Emrick and Peterson, 1978; Giacquinta, 1973; Goodlad, 1975; Havelock, 1971; Reutter, 1979.)

● The source of the idea for staff involvement does not matter; what matters most is how people are organized; whether the people who maintain leadership are sensitive to change and teachers' realities; and whether commitment, rewards, and support can be sustained long enough for teachers to integrate them or enhance their repertoire.

(Daft and Becker, Bentzen, Emrick, Loucks, and Peterson, 1983; Sieber, 1979.)

● The process of implementation—that is, actually doing something different in the classroom and finding it to be more effective—is the critical process for teachers.

(Berman, 1979; Berman and McLaughlin, 1978; Farrar and others, 1979; Fullan, 1977; McLaughlin and Marsh, 1978.)

References

Austin, Gilbert R. "Exemplary Schools and the Search for Effectiveness." *Educational Leadership* 37, 1 (October 1979): 10–14.

Baldridge, J.V., and Deal, Terence. *Managing Change in Educational Organization.* Berkeley, Calif.: McCutchan Publishers, 1975.

Barth, Roland, *Open Education and the American School.* New York: Agathan Press, 1972.

Bentzen, Mary M. *Changing Schools: The Magic Feather Principle.* New York: McGraw-Hill, 1974.

Berlak, Ann, and Berlak, Harold. *The Dilemmas of Schooling.* London: Metheun & Co., Ltd., 1981.

Berman, Paul. "Toward an Implementation Paradigm of Educational Change." Paper prepared for the National Institute of Education, October 1979.

Berman, Paul, and McLaughlin, Milbrey. *Federal Programs Supporting Educational Change, Volume III.* Santa Monica, Calif.: The Rand Corporation, 1978.

Bidwell, Charles. "The School as a Formal Organization." In *Handbook of Organizations.* Chicago: Rand McNally and Co., 1965.

Brookover, W., and Lezotte, Lawrence W. "Changes in School Characteristics Coincident with Change in Student Achievement." East Lansing: Institute for Research on Teaching, Michigan State University, 1979.

Burlingame, Martin. "Some Neglected Dimensions in the Study of Educational Administration." *Educational Administration Quarterly* 15, 1 (Winter 1979): 1–18.

Bussis, Anne M.; Chittenden, Edward; and Amarel, Marianne. *Beyond Surface Curriculum: An Interview Study of Teachers' Understandings.* Boulder: Westview Press, 1976.

Charter, W.W. *Measuring the Implementation of Differentiated Staffing.* Eugene, Ore.: Center for Advanced Study of Educational Administration, 1973.

Clark, David; Lotto, Linda; and McCarthy, M. "Factors Associated with Success in Urban Elementary Schools." *Phi Delta Kappan* (March 1980).

Clark, David L.; McKibbin, Sue; and Malkas, Mark, eds. *Alternative Perspectives for Viewing Educational Organizations.* San Francisco: Far West Laboratory, 1981.

Cox, Pat L. "Complementary Roles in Successful Change." *Educational Leadership* 41, 3 (November 1983): 10–13.

Corwin, Ronald. *Reform and Organizational Survival: The Teacher Corps as an Instrument of Educational Change.* New York: Wiley Interscience, 1973.

Crandall, David P., and associates. *People, Policies, and Practices: Examining the Chain of School Improvement.* Andover, Mass.: The Network, 1982.

Culver, C., and Hoban, G. *The Power to Change: Issues for the Innovative Educator.* New York: McGraw-Hill, 1973.

Daft, Richard, and Becker, Selwyn. The Innovative Organization. New York: Elsevier, 1978.

Deal, Terence, and Celotti, Lynn D. "Loose Coupling and the School Administrator: Some Recent Research Findings." Stanford: Center for Research and Development in Teaching, Stanford University, 1977.

Denham, C., and Lieberman, A. *Time to Learn*. Washington, D.C.: National Institute of Education, 1980.

Dreeben, Robert. *The Nature of Teaching*. Glenview, Ill.: Scott, Foresman & Co., 1970.

Edmonds, Ron. "An Address to the Teacher Corps." Speech delivered in Washington, D.C., August 1978.

Elmore, Richard, and McLaughlin, Milbrey. "Strategic Choice in Federal Education Policy; The Compliance-Assistance Trade Off." In *The Complexities of Policy Making in Education*. Eighty-first yearbook of the National Society for the Study of Education. Edited by A. Lieberman and M. McLaughlin. Chicago: University of Chicago Press, 1982.

Emrich, John, and Peterson, Susan. *A Synthesis of Findings Across Five Recent Studies in Educational Dissemination and Change*. San Francisco: Far West Laboratory, 1978.

Farrar, Eleanor; DeSanctis, John E.; and Cohen, David K. "Views From Below: Implementation Research in Education." Cambridge, Mass.: Huron Institute, 1979.

Feitler, Fred. "Bureaucratic Myths: Does Loose Couplingi Go Far Enough?" Paper delivered before the American Educational Research Association, Boston, April 1980.

Field, Kristin. *Teacher Development: A Study of Stages in the Development of Teachers*. Brookline, Mass.: Teacher Center, 1979.

Fullan, Michael, and Pomfret, A. "Research on Curriculum and Instruction Implementation." *Review of Educational Research* 47, 1 (Winter 1977): 335–397.

Fullan, Michael. *The Meaning of Educational Change*. New York: Teachers College Press, 1982.

Giacquinta, Joseph. "The Process of Organizational Change in Schools." In *Review of Research in Education*. Edited by F. Derlinger. Itasca, Ill.: F.E. Peacock, Inc., 1973.

Gibson, Troy. *Teachers Talking—Aims, Methods, Attitudes to Change*. London: Allen Love, 1973.

Gold, Barry, and Miles, M. *Whose School is it Anyway?* New York: Proeger, 1981.

Goodlad, John I. *Dynamics of Educational Change*. New York: McGraw-Hill, 1975.

Goodlad, John I. *A Place Called School*. New York: McGraw-Hill, 1984.

Grace, Gerald. *Teachers, Ideaology and Control: A Study in Urban Education*. Boston: Routledge and Kegan Paul, 1978.

Griffiths, Daniel E. "Intellectual Turmoil in Educational Administration." Address before the American Educational Research Association, San Francisco, 1979.

Gross, Neal; Giacquinta, J.; and Bernstein, M. *Implementing Organizational Innovations*. New York: Basic Books, 1971.

Hall, Gene, and Loucks, Susan. "Teacher Concerns as a Basis for Facilitating and Personalizing Staff Development." In *Staff Development: New Demands, New Realities, New Perspectives*. Edited by A. Lieberman and L. Miller. New York: Teachers College Press, 1979.

Havelock, Ronald. "Planning for Innovation Through Dissemination and Utilization of Knowledge." Ann Arbor: Center for Research on Utilization of Scientific Knowledge, University of Michigan, 1971.

Heath, Douglas. *Humanizing Schools: New Directions, New Decisions*. Rochelle Park, N.J.: Hayden, 1971.

Heath, Douglas. *Maturity and Competence: A Transcultural View*. New York: Garner (Division of Wiley), 1977.

House, Ernest. *The Politics of Educational Innovation*. Berkeley, Calif.: McCutchan Publishing, 1974.

Huberman, A., and Miles, Michael, with Beverly Loy Taylor and Jo Ann Goldberg. *Innovation Up Close: A Field Study in Twelve School Settings*. Andover, Mass.: The Network, 1982.

Huff, Anne W. "Planning to Plan." In *New Perspectives on Planning in Educational Organizations*. Edited by David Clark. San Francisco: Far West Laboratory, 1979.

Jackson, P. *Life in Classrooms*. New York: Holt, Rinehart & Winston, 1968.

Katz, Daniel, and Kahn, Robert L. *The Social Psychology of Organizations*. New York: John Wiley and Sons, 1966.

Kepler, Karen B. "B.T.E.S. Implications for Pre-Service Education of Teachers." In *Time to Learn*. Edited by C. Denham and A. Lieberman. Washington, D.C.: National Institute of Education, 1980.

Lewin, Kurt. "Frontiers in Group Dynamics: Concept, Method and Reality in Social Science, Social Equilibria and Social Change." *Human Relations* 1, 1 (June 1947).

Lieberman, Ann, and Shiman, David. "The Stages of Change in Elementary School Settings." In *The Power to Change*. Edited by C. Culver and G. Hoban. New York: McGraw-Hill, 1973.

Lieberman, Ann. "The Effects of Principal Leadership on Teacher Morale, Professionalism and Style in the Classroom." Doctoral dissertation, University of California at Los Angeles, 1969.

Lieberman, Ann, and Miller, Lynne. "Supporting Classroom Change." In *Changing School Mathematics: A Responsive Process*. Reston, Va.: National Council of Teachers of Mathematics, in press.

Lightfoot, Sara Lawrence. "The Lives of Teachers." In *Handbook of Teaching and Policy*. Edited by L.S. Shulman and G. Sykes. New York: Longman, 1983.

Lipham, James. "The Administrator's Role in Educational Linkage." In *Linking Processes in Educational Improvement*. Edited by N. Nash and J. Culbertson. Columbus, Ohio: University Council for Educational Administration, 1977.

Lortie, Dan. *School Teacher*. Chicago: University of Chicago Press, 1975.

Lortie, Dan. "School Teachers and Their Principals." Speech before the Metropolitan School Study Council conference at Wave Hill, Riverside, New York, November 1983.

Loucks, Susan F. "At Last: Some Good News From a Study of School Improvement." *Educational Leadership* 41, 3 (November 1983): 4–5.

Maiocco, Donald. "Effects of Principal Leadership Style on the Social Grouping of Teachers." Doctoral dissertation, Teachers College, Columbia University, 1978.

Majone, Giandomenico, and Wildavsky, Aaron. "Implementation as Evolution: Exorcising the Ghosts in the Implementation Machine." Russell Sage Discussion Papers, No. 2.

Mann, Dale. "The Politics and Administration of the Instructionally Effective School." Boston: AERA, 1980.

Mcpherson, Gertrude. *Small Town Teacher.* Cambridge: Harvard University Press, 1972.

Meyer, John. "Research on School and District Organization." Paper presented at the Sociology of Education conference, San Diego, 1977.

Meyer, John, and Rowan, Brian. "Institutionalized Organizations: Formal Structure as Myth and Ceremony." *American Journal of Sociology* 83, 2.

Miles, Matthew B. "Some Properties of Schools as Social Systems." In *Change in School Systems.* Edited by G. Watson. Washington, D.C.: National Training Laboratories, National Education Association, 1967.

Miles, Matthew B. "Unraveling the Mystery of Institutionalization." *Educational Leadership* 41, 3 (November 1983): 14–19.

Miles, Matthew B. "Common Properties of Schools in Context: The Backdrop for Knowledge Utilization and School Improvement." Prepared for Program on Research and Educational Practice. Washington, D.C.: National Institute of Education, 1979.

Purkey, Stewart C., and Smith, Marshall S. "Too Soon to Cheer? Synthesis of Research on Effective Schools." *Educational Leadership* 40, 3 (December, 1982): 64–69.

Popkowitz, Thomas; Tabachnick, B.; and Wehlage, G. *The Myth of Educational Reform.* Madison: University of Wisconsin Press, 1982.

Reutter, Michael, and others. *Fifteen Thousand Hours: Secondary Schools and Their Effects on Children.* Cambridge: Harvard University Press, 1979.

Sarason, Seymour. *The Cultures of the School and the Problem of Change.* Boston: Allyn and Bacon, 1971.

Schlecty, Phillip C. *Teaching and Social Behavior.* Boston: Allyn and Bacon, 1976.

Schmuck, Richard; Runkel, Philip; and others. *Handbook of Organization Development in Schools.* Eugene: Center for Advanced Study of Educational Administration, University of Oregon, 1972.

Sieber, Sam. "Organizational Influences on Innovative Roles." In *Managing Change in Organizations.* Edited by J.A. Balderidge and T. Deal. Berkeley: McCutchan, 1975.

Sieber, Sam. "Incentives and Disincentives for Knowledge Utilization in Public Education." Paper prepared for the Program on Research and Educational Practice. Washington, D.C.: National Institute of Education, 1979.

Smith, Lou, and Keith, Pat. *Anatomy of Educational Innovation.* New York: John Wiley and Sons, 1971.

Sprinthall, Norman, and Mosher, Ralph, eds. *Value Development as the Aim in Education.* Schenectady, N.Y.: Character Research Press, 1978.

Squires, David. "Characteristics of Effective Schools: The Importance of School Processes." Philadelphia: Research for Better Schools, 1980.

Sussman, Leila. *Tales Out of School.* Philadelphia: Temple University Press, 1977.

Waller, Willard. *The Sociology of Teaching.* New York: John Wiley and Sons, 1967.

Weick, Karl. "Educational Organizations as Loosely Coupled Systems." In *Administrative Science Quarterly* 21 (March 1976).

Williams, Richard D., and others. *Effecting Organizational Renewal in Schools.* New York: McGraw-Hill, 1974.

Wolcott, Harry. *Teachers vs. Technocrats.* Eugene: Center for Educational Policy and Management, University of Oregon, 1977.

Zaltman, G.; Florio, D.; and Sikorski, L. *Dynamic Educational Change.* New York: Free Press, 1977.

6

The Content of School Improvement: Thinking, Organizing, and Acting

But we feel that both theory and practice of
education have suffered in the past
from an overattention to what ought to be and
its correlative tendency to disregard what is.
When theory is not based upon existing
practice, a great hiatus appears between
theory and practice, and the consequence
is that the progressiveness of theory does not
affect the conservatism of practice.

—Willard Waller, 1967

In this chapter, we explore other issues relating to school improvement and discuss how to provide for the continuing growth of
teachers in a way that uses what we know about (1) teachers as adult
learners, (2) strategies and substance for organizing, and (3) realities of
the teacher.

The teacher's intentions will inevitably be affected by the assumptions s/he makes
regarding human nature and human possibility. Many of these assumptions are
hidden: Most have never been articulated. If s/he is to achieve clarity and full

consciousness, the teacher must attempt to make such assumptions explicit, for only then can they be examined, analyzed and understood (Greene, 1973).

Teachers as Adult Learners

Studies about adult development provide us with a useful framework for dealing with school improvement. They help us to see teachers as differentiated on many dimensions. (See Figures 5 and 6, pages 140–142).

Field (1979) describes what many teachers feel intuitively—that teachers gain control of their professional lives through experience. Teachers move through stages. At stage one, teachers do not have a feel for how to move the class along. They are mechanical, often tight in their plans. Later on, as they stick with it and enter stage two, teachers experience enough success to relax somewhat, to see students as capable of working on their own at times, to see learning as more continuous— more than just moving from one assignment to the other. At stage three teachers can feel and act upon a sense of experimentation and minimal threat. They learn wherever they are. They pick up ideas from supermarkets, TV, friends, even from a poor class. They see the classroom as an integrated whole.

This information helps us see teachers as having different capacities and understandings of the classroom and heightens our sensitivity to individual variation. Just as we ask teachers to look at students both as a group and as individuals, so we ask school improvers to view teachers as a collective and as unique. This kind of thinking encourages the notion of teacher differences.

Bussis, Chittenden, and Amarel's (1976) work gives a refinement on how teachers meet the cognitive and social needs of their students and of themselves. They present a picture of how different priorities lead teachers to different kinds of concerns; for instance, teachers with narrow cognitive and social priorities stress facts, the basic skills, and students "being good." If we want to move these teachers to broader priorities, we must provide experiences where they can see students taking more responsibility, perhaps being given a choice, or in some way learning in a less controlled environment. Bussis, Chittenden, and Amarel help us to see teacher development as movement from total teacher control to consideration of the learners' purposes and their perspectives as a consideration. Teachers with comprehensive priorities are like Field's stage three teachers. They know how to provide for basic skills, but they also incorporate independent learning and the possibility for shared decisions between teacher and student.

Harvey, Hunt, and Shroder (1961) describe another developmental view of teachers. They indicate a movement from a dependence on authority, to struggling with conflict, to being open to new ways of thinking, to full-scale cooperation. We can see that the notion of external authority, whether expressed in terms of Bussis' narrow concerns or Field's stage one teacher, reveals a pattern that is tight, controlling, and probably fearful of ambiguity. Stage theories alert us to a dynamic view of teachers and their possibilities for growth; they look for a match of where teachers are in terms of what they know, what they see as important, and what occupies their major work concerns.

Perhaps the best-known translation of a developmental scheme for understanding teachers is Hall and Louck's (1979) stages of concern. Observing teachers in a variety of settings, these authors have built a scale that moves from little concern ("This innovation has nothing to do with us.") to increased concern and action. For example, faced with ideas new to them, teachers often fear they will not be adequate to the task, or they may reject an idea if adequate support is not forthcoming. As personal concerns recede, management concerns ("How do I actually do this in my classroom?") begin to dominate. Actual demonstrations or in-class help are being called for. This stage leads teachers to question whether a new program is better than the old ("Are children learning more taking out more books, reading more, etc.?"). Teachers apparently only feel comfortable collaborating when they are comfortable with the innovation. Hall and Loucks provide a tool for gathering information that may be useful in planning inservice activities to support school improvement efforts.

Looking at teachers along developmental lines can give us clues about what we can do to enhance growth, as well as describe it. Heath's (1977) and Sprinthall and Mosher's (1978) works attempt to do just that. They provide direction for enhancing teachers' learning and enlightenment. They sensitize us to the critical elements of adult developmental theory.

We may make some general statements about teachers based on the literature on adult development. Among them:

• Teaching can be viewed as having many components. It is possible to be at one stage of development on behavioral issues and at another on curriculum problems (Field, 1979).

• Teachers differ on what they pay attention to and how much experience they have had with a variety of learners, materials, and contexts.

• Focusing on growth, rather than remediation, allows for alternatives and enhancement rather than threat.

• By paying attention to the content of developmental theory, teaching, and interpersonal relationships, one may design strategies that affect teachers (Oja and Sprinthall, 1978).

Strategies and Substance for Organizing

From a framework of adult development, we can move to a better understanding of some specific modes of organizing for change. We recognize that teachers do their work in a specific social context and that the context can provide and influence teacher growth. Therefore, both the process and the substance of school improvement activities must attend to the particulars of the situation. There are many ways to engage a school staff.

In the Beginning

To introduce any new project, idea, or mandate, there are some solid experiences from which we can draw. Awareness activities can be used. For example:

Visitations—Teachers rarely visit other classrooms even though we know that much learning goes on among peers. Many teachers respond negatively to visits. ("I can't do that in my classroom." But even that negative response seems to mean that there is some reflection going on. There is an awareness.)

"Informal" discussion—We often respond better in discussions that take place in a less formal atmosphere. Challenging one's teaching in a formal speech is hard to accept, and the substance gets lost with the process.

Hands-on experientially related substance—This could be actually creating curricula or materials, but it also has an intellectual component. For instance, teachers may hear that "the more time-on-task, the more students learn." A common response is, "So what! That's obvious." But we also know that the obvious often is not practiced, so the problem is to create experiential learning that helps teachers reflect on what they're doing (Smyth, 1980). Using the time-on-task research, teachers can *initially* discuss:

- Mastery vs. coverage
- Whole-class, small-group, and individual instruction
- Teacher decisions, joint decisions, child decisions
- Needs of individuals and needs of the group
- Time allocated to various subjects (Kepler, 1982).

These are all issues that represent dilemmas for many teachers, and all deal with time as a critical component. There is no one answer to these dilemmas, but they unlock the kinds of problems that teachers rarely share.

Challenge and choice—Treating teachers as experts or adult learners continuously requires activities that are both challenging and allow for choice—challenging because teaching lends itself to continuous reflection, and providing choice because different teaching styles produce different kinds of results. For instance, for an initial inservice day, teachers could be given a choice between three activities: participating in a panel discussion, observing a demonstration lesson, or becoming learners in an inquiry lesson. The teacher can opt for one of three roles, that of learner, observer, or participant among peers. If the theme were inquiry, time-on-task, or "enhancing one's repertoire," the challenge of better understanding one's teaching becomes the content.

But challenge and choice alone are not enough. Content without follow-up opportunities for in-class practice, feedback, and encouragement—those same practices that teachers should provide for children—are important for teachers, too. In short, we need not only content, but a mode of delivering the content as well (Stallings, 1981).

Content That Helps Teachers Reflect on What They are Doing and Why

Certainly part of the content of school improvement are ideas that can help teachers look at what they are doing and make changes when they find that those changes can enhance their teaching repertoire. There are many ways to do this. We describe several different modes to show that substance and process, when effective, are intricately woven together.

The Discovery Method

Gibson describes a method of experiential learning for teachers that allows them to work on a common theme in a nonthreatening way in their own classrooms.

1. First, a theme was chosen. Teachers were asked to consider conditions under which unfamiliar ideas would be used in the classroom. The concept of "Living Space" was the organizing focus. The question, what would be needed to kindle interest in the class on this theme, was asked.

2. Teachers were encouraged to try something they didn't ordinarily do. The trial period was to be one hour. (That is those who only taught to the whole group, tried small-group activities. Some tried students working on a project together.)

3. The theme of Living Space allowed teachers to come up with different teaching versions of how to deal with the topic (e.g., posing questions, designing a house, opinion polls, poems, stories).

4. Teachers who normally used group project methods tried whole class teaching. Those who usually did whole class teaching tried project methods.

5. This experiment opened teachers to new ways of organizing and thinking about their class and involved them in different types of activities. By force of circumstance, teachers discover for themselves that some of the most effective ways of learning depend not so much on techniques, or bodies of knowledge, as on relationships (Gibson, 1973, pp. 265–67).

Local Problem Solving

Sometimes engagement in a problem that is common to a group of teachers is sufficient substance for organizing and mobilizing teachers in their own behalf. The case that follows, based on a situation in an urban high school in 1981, illustrates such an example.

An Administrator's Strategy

One of the things I decided to do when I got to Johnson High School was to spend some time "hanging out" in the teachers' lounges and lunch room. I kept hearing about how teachers were not "backed up" on issues of discipline and attendance. When I pushed to find out what "backed up" meant, I was told that administrators weren't tough enough or consistent, seemed to close their eyes to kids in the halls during class time, and just didn't listen to teachers' complaints. The almost intuitive response to this from "progressive educators" is to dismiss teachers as being conservative. In fact, many of the teachers had been told not to "whine" so much about attendance, that the best way to improve attendance is to improve instruction—make class so interesting that kids rush to get there. This reaction made teachers feel unacknowledged and dismissed.

However, I soon discovered there was some truth to complaints about the halls. After the bell had rung, there were a number of students in the halls just roaming around, in the lavatories, or in the library (not reading, often playing cards). A lot of these students were minorities or kids who were "school alienated" in some way. It struck me that no one was doing these kids any favors by letting them roam the halls. I also discovered that the teachers' concern for attendance and "back up" was almost obsessive. It seemed to be an issue that deserved attention; that if it weren't attended to, there would be no hope of getting to what I consider more interesting issues of instruction, learning, curriculum, and teaching.

We initiated an attendance committee that consisted of ten teachers and myself. Meeting once a week at 7:30 in the morning, we divided our task, more or less, into these parts:

- Define the problem
- Research the problem
- Come up with some alternative solutions
- Decide on what appears to be the best solution
- Explain the solution to other teachers
- Implement a new policy.

In defining the problem, we decided that the issue was in letting students know that we wanted them to be in class and to be there on time; that we were concerned about their learning; and that we had simple expectations that, if not met, carried some consequences. We researched the problem by asking each teacher to submit the names of all students who had more than five unexcused absences over a three-week period. When we plotted out these absences on a bar graph, we found that only 30 students were out all day long and that the others "skipped" only specific classes. We also found that most student absences occurred during the first hour, the lunch hours, and at the end of the day. We knew, then, that the problem with absences was not an all-day problem, but a period-by-period problem. And we knew which periods were most troublesome. We also found out that tardiness was a problem equal to skipping, that students often entered class as much as 30 minutes late; that most of them felt no need to hurry to class; and that, to accommodate this situation, many teachers didn't get down to business until ten to 15 minutes had elapsed. That meant that instructional time was considerably diminished. It had become acceptable to be late and to spend less time on instruction.

We next categorized our concerns as minimum rules that were needed and consequences for not meeting the rules. Some teachers on the committee solicited faculty opinion from the whole staff through a questionnaire. Again, we heard, "be consistent." We also heard a lot of cynicism that there was nothing we could do; that it had all been tried before; and that nothing works. In addition, there was a majority opinion that attendance was the concern of the administration; instruction was the concern of the teacher. (Yet attendance was a real obsession and presented a neat contradiction: "I don't care—I do care.")

The committee came up with two very basic and almost embarrassingly simple rules: (1) we expect all students to go to class when they are not legitimately absent; and (2) we expect all students to go to class on time. We also made it clear that it was every teacher's and administrator's responsibility to enforce these rules, and that without cooperation, the policy would indeed fail. Tardies were to be made up in time with the teacher at his or her convenience or during the lunch hour in a supervised study hall. We devised the following steps to handle attendance:

1. After three unexcused absences, the teacher in the missed class prepares a home contract.

2. After five unexcused absences, the teacher refers the student's name to the administration, who follows up on the student through the department of pupil personnel.

3. Students who accumulate five or more illegitimate absences may be expected to make up all work missed before being readmitted to class. This work may be completed in a supervised study hall.

We waited until the winter semester began to introduce the policy. First, we met with small groups of teachers during their prep periods to explain the policy and procedures; to highlight problems we hadn't considered; and, very importantly, to ask the teachers to volunteer their support by being out in the halls, offering to escort late students to class, and letting it be known that all staff were concerned about kids getting to class. We explained the policy to the students by handing out copies of the rules and consequences in each first-hour class, having the teacher go over the rules, asking the kids to sign a statement saying they understood the rules, and having this backed up with a statement by the principal.

From the first day, the results were phenomenal. Almost every teacher in the school was out in the halls. They were friendly and walked students to class, encountering little if any resistence. In fact, many teachers commented that the kids liked the attention and jokingly asked to be "escorted to class." Many teachers, too, liked being in the halls and interacting with students in an informal way outside of the classroom. More importantly, it made them feel they had taken back some of the authority they had lost somewhere along the line.

After two weeks, it was acknowledged that the policy was working. The attendance committee still continues to meet and hold open meetings with staff, and to put out a weekly bulletin to faculty members. Some days are worse than

*others, but on the whole there is a measurably different atmosphere in the build-
ing—one that is characterized less by oppressiveness and control (as one might
expect or fear) and more by respect for teaching and learning, social responsibility,
and cooperation. We have managed to identify which students have the most
problem with attendance. Usually, they come meandering in after nine weeks
asking to be allowed to return to classes they have never attended. Our plan is
to identify these kids by the end of the third week and contact them about what
they are doing. The study hall will provide a way for them to catch up and re-
enter class. It is clear that we have only solved part of the problem, but there is
more here than meets the eye:*

* *Teachers feel some sense of colleagueship with each other; they have united*
to do something *rather than* making do *on their own in isolation.*

* *Teachers feel supported by the administration, rather than blamed for the
problems in the school. And lines of communication between the administration
and teachers have been opened.*

* *There is a shared sense that the adults in a school do have authority that
they can use in constructive ways. Many teachers felt their authority had been
greatly undermined in the past ten years or so. They've discovered it again.*

* *The students have supported the policy; the student newspaper even ran
an editorial in favor of it.*

* *Teachers were involved in making the policy and in implementing it.
Some took leadership positions and gently cajoled others into helping out. It was
clearly viewed as a teacher effort.*

* *The attendance issue and how we dealt with it provided a framework and
a starting place for future staff development efforts focused on instruction and
curriculum.*

Most important, we began where teachers *saw the problem, not where I
saw it or where the experts, supervisors, saw it. Together, we became engaged
in a concrete issue that was seriously affecting the smooth running of the school,
bringing down faculty morale, and blocking the potential for having a school
where "learning is the top priority." This effort took five months.*

If we look closely at this case, we can unravel many of the complexities we have referred to as understandings and can see how, in subtle
ways, distrust of the faculty, our own expectations, and our absence
from the dailiness cloud how we work with teachers.

The teachers were saying that they had a problem (attendance). For
a long time the problem was discarded. Implication: "It's your fault,"
"the problem isn't important," "teachers aren't good enough, that's why

students cut class," "teachers like to complain." "They" don't really want to deal with the big issues (instruction).

The administrator attempted to use a rational process to discover how to solve the problem. At last, someone took the teachers seriously. And we see a process begin.

- Teachers' definition of a problem is respected.
- A team meets to decide on strategy (cooperation).
- Evidence is collected (problem is better understood).
- Action plans are drawn.
- Everyone is involved (meetings with teachers; students and principal are informed).
- Teachers pay attention to students in the hall.
- Teachers monitor the process.
- Students get more attention from the teachers.
- High expectations for attendance are built.
- A feeling of caring is initiated, which translates to the building of a school "ethos."

We use this example because of our belief that what matters most is that local efforts start where the teachers help define the problem—not what looks good or what should be a problem. This is only the start of a long process, building experience in defining problems and taking collective action.

Research Transformed Into Usable Improved Practices

Sometimes the content and strategies for implementation start directly with research findings. But those findings are only real for teachers when the referent is their own classroom. Several are described here—an example of an outside group taking direct instruction findings and working them through the workshop way of learning in a high school; a focus on mastery learning and the creation of innovative norms in elementary and junior high schools; a research and development group designing and implementing teaching behaviors *and* staff development strategies; and the American Federation of Teachers creating both a new role (teacher-research linker) and activities based on research.

Changing Teacher Behavior (Stallings, 1981)

Stallings, over the last several years, has demonstrated that one can take research findings and develop a system for using those findings. The content in this instance is research on reading where several descriptive variables were found to be related to higher reading scores. These variables included:

- Discussing or reviewing seatwork or homework
- Instructing new work
- Drill and practice
- Students reading aloud
- Focusing instruction on a small group or total group
- Praise and support of success
- Positive corrective feedback
- Short quizzes.

These findings do not move most teachers because they seem to be so commonplace. The problem is to provide *engagement for teachers* that helps them reflect on the degree to which they are "with it" (Kounin, 1970)[1] and to provide continuous experiential activities that encourage trying out new ways of doing things in the classroom.

Techniques are enabling. One might say that a mastery of group management techniques enables a teacher to be free from concern about management (Kounin, 1970, p. 145).

Stallings took the findings and created an observational checklist for teachers (Stallings, 1981, p. 32), which serves as the beginning of a series of workshops in which teachers receive their own profile (based on observation) of how they are doing on a number of classroom variables such as teacher praise and feedback. Several workshops focus on specific techniques for changing specific behaviors. Role-playing, specific incidents, and discussion of students serve as the content, and workshops serve as the process for working with a small group of teachers in remedial reading. Some key ingredients for improvement are practiced:

- Personalized feedback is given to the teachers (individual profile).
- Research findings are translated to classroom activities.
- Teachers are confronted (that is, challenged with specific ways of improving their teaching).
- Workshops focus on specific techniques and subject matter that allow for concentrated activities.
- Small groups provide for supportive, informal arrangements.

---

[1]"Withitness" was observed by Kounin to describe such activities as (a) the teacher's knowing what is going on regarding children's behavior (attending to several things at the same time); (b) managing movement and transitions; (c) keeping the group on focus; (d) challenging arousal; and (e) knowing how to keep the class involved.

- Experiential learning comes from each teacher's own classroom.
- Workshops consider starting with a structure (external authority) and moving developmentally with teachers as they begin to work on their own improvement possibilities.

Mastery Learning: Collegiality and Experimentation (Little, 1981)

In still another example, a group of schools began working on mastery learning as a technique for improving reading skills in elementary and junior high schools. Little reports on a year-long study of these schools in an attempt to understand in more precise terms how a small district staff development group helped provide the support for mastery learning. Her in-depth study helps describe in specific terms the growth of two powerful norms that characterize successful schools—collegiality and experimentation. She describes the powerful necessity for supportive social arrangements *as well as* technical knowledge. (One without the other does not consider the interplay of skills and the capacity and ability to learn on the part of individuals with daily supportive social conditions.) Group *and* individual needs are both considered and the interplay is described.

Little's painstaking observation and analysis begins to unlock the catch words like "climate," "support," "trust" by describing how they come about, what actions produce "adaptability," how teachers and principal go about their daily activities. She begins by describing four critical practices of successful schools.[2]

- *Teachers talk about practice.* They begin to build a shared language about what they are doing. The focus is off children per se and on the substance, process, interactions, and so forth. The focus is on practice, not teachers.
- *Teachers and administrators plan, design, research, evaluate, and prepare materials together.* It is in the interaction of ideas, plans, and execution that people become committed.[3]
- *Teachers and administrators observe each other working.* Colleagueship in a collective struggle is more apt than evaluation and control.
- *Teachers and administrators teach each other the practice of teaching.* The resources of the school are recognized and encouraged. As many as

---

[2]Her definition includes those schools that successfully implemented mastery learning and where the norms of collegiality and experimentation were firmly implanted.

[3]Such a process was described earlier as D(ialog), D(ecisionmaking), A(ction), and E(valuation)—DDAE—in Bentzen (1974), *Improving Schools: The Magic Feather Principle*.

possible share their resources with each other—not just ditto sheets, but past and current learnings.

Little draws our attention to the subtleties of "relevant interaction" as opposed to "demanding" interaction (that is, discussions that hit the tough issues that teachers face *as they understand them*). Her critical practices of successful schools give us the specifics of content and process in school improvement, such as those listed in the following inventory (Little, 1981, p. 13).

Inventory of Characteristic Teacher Interactions in Six Schools
- Design and prepare materials
- Design curriculum units
- Research materials and ideas for curriculum
- Write curriculum
- Prepare lesson plans
- Review and discuss plans
- Credit new ideas and programs
- Persuade others to try an idea
- Make collective agreements to test an idea
- Invite others to observe
- Observe other teachers
- Analyze practices and effects
- Teach others in formal inservice
- Teach others informally
- Talk "publicly about what one is learning"
- Convert book chapters to reflect new approach (transforming ideas to action)
- Design in-service
- Evaluate performance of principals.

These practices involve the key ingredients of publicly setting the expectations for colleagueship through action (teaching with each other, inviting others to observe, making collective agreements to test ideas, and so forth) and at the same time encouraging experimentation. Needless to say, Little focuses, too, on the critical importance of the role of the principal in modeling collegiality and encouraging a range of activities while maintaining focus on staff development activities.

The Changing Teacher Practice Study (Griffin and others, 1983)

Another example of using research findings as a means of intervention was carried out by the Research in Teacher Education (RITE) program area of the Research and Development Center for Teacher Education. The Changing Teacher Practice study was designed and implemented to demonstrate a cost effective and efficient way to introduce research-derived leadership and teaching into a school district. Two bodies of research were examined to select teaching and leadership strategies that were consistently reported as being "effective." The results of this examination were a set of teaching behaviors (Barnes, 1981) and a set of staff development strategies (Edwards, 1981):

Teaching Behaviors
1. Learning environment (warm and supportive)
2. Classroom management (well organized)
3. Classroom instruction (work oriented)
4. Productive use of time (brisk pacing)
5. Specific behaviors included:
   a. Gaining student attention
   b. Clear presentation
   c. Practice of new skills
   d. Monitoring
   e. Providing feedback
   f. Assigning individual seatwork
   g. Evaluating student responses

Staff Development Strategies
1. Teacher interaction on professional issues
2. Technical assistance to teachers
3. Adaptation of ideas to "fit" school and classroom regularities
4. Opportunities for reflection
5. Focused and precise substance

This information, along with supporting materials, was synthesized into a 23-hour intervention presented to experimental group principals and resource teachers (staff developers) in a large urban district. The district was not without problems in that it had experienced many of the typical school issues of the 80s (decreasing support, budget constraints, court-ordered provision of equal opportunity, and so on). The intervention was conducted over five consecutive days prior to the opening of the 82–83 school year. Both staff developers and teachers reported their interactions with each other. Students were observed for on- or off-task behavior.

The experimental group staff developers demonstrated twice as many research-based strategies than did the control group staff developers. Second, there was a significant difference in favor of the experimental group teachers in terms of research-based teaching acts. Third, there was a significant difference in favor of the experimental group students' on-task behavior.

The district felt so strongly about the results of this study that it adopted it for all 175 of its elementary and middle schools.

Educational Research and Dissemination Program (ER&D) (Biles and others, 1983)

The American Federation of Teachers (AFT) has developed still another way of transforming research for teacher use. In three sites throughout the country, the AFT selected local coordinators to work on the ER&D project. Teacher Research Linkers, selected at building sites, are people viewed by teachers as innovative and task-oriented risk takers who combine personal strengths in working with people and professional strengths as teachers. These people, representing an "on-site" resource, know how to use research focused on classroom management and effective teaching strategies. During the project, which lasted two years, a resource manual was developed (Biles and others, 1983) that includes materials describing the training of the Teacher Research Linkers and the various activities that were developed in working with teachers to transform research findings into activities. The research is summarized, and appropriate activities that illuminate the research and attend to teacher classroom realities are presented. The research topics include effective classroom management for the beginning of the school year, effective group management practices, teacher praise, and direct instruction or interactive teaching. Included with the resource manual is a collection of easy-to-read articles on the research topics.

This project has involved teachers in reading the research, making it meaningful to them, and establishing a new role to involve teachers in using the research. Most importantly, the process described by ER&D can be used in any school building.

Thus we are beginning to build a set of principles that incorporates the variations among teachers and their interactions in teachers' own social contexts. Influential staff development now begins to be characterized by:

- *A developmental nature,* allowing for teacher variation.
- *Practicality,* allowing for the concrete application of ideas (Smyth, 1980; Little, 1981).
- *Interaction,* allowing for teacher-principal as well as teacher-teacher relationships.
- *Role variation,* allowing teachers and principals to be learners, teachers, models, and supporters.

- *Continuity*, allowing for focus on a theme and time enough to take hold.
- *An attractive focus* that is important, engaging, and far-reaching.
- *Personalization*, allowing for informality and formality connected to personal involvement.

These characteristics are obviously easier to describe than to facilitate, partly because we are telescoping the amount of time involved in building a healthy, open, collaborative school and partly because organizations look more like a knotted string as the interaction of people moves between periods of stability and turbulence (Huff, 1981).

Sometimes process and substance for staff improvement can come about by the actual engagement of teachers in the research process itself.

Concurrent Research and Development

Most of the study of what should be kept in schools and what should go and what should be added must be done in hundreds of thousands of classrooms and thousands of American communities. The studies must be undertaken by those who may have to change the way they do things as a result of the studies. Our schools cannot keep up with the life they are supposed to sustain and improve unless teachers, pupils, supervisors, and school patrons continuously examine what they are doing (Corey, 1953, p. viii).

Action Research Revisited

Over 30 years ago, under the auspices of the Horace Mann Lincoln Institute at Teachers College, Columbia University, a group of university people worked with several different school districts in a collaborative research effort. The research differed from traditional research in that the emphasis and substance of the research problem was identified by the school people themselves, with the help of a university researcher. A traditional research process was imposed upon a school problem. An example described by Corey (1953) helps us see how the content comes about and what the process looks like as it is enacted.

A. IDENTIFYING THE PROBLEM

A particular school has a curriculum committee that works on subject area. The group complains that they never get anything accomplished because (1) the meetings are not worthwhile; (2) members take no responsibility for the success of meetings; (3) the leader is overburdened; and (4) no one seems to carry through on decisions. To make sure that this is indeed a problem the group cares about, the impressions are checked out by informal interviews. Not only are concerns revealed, but a checksheet is prepared for the improvement of meetings.

B. PREPARING THE ACTION HYPOTHESIS
   Two hypotheses are created for testing:
   1. Limiting the leader to . . .
      a. Clarifying statements
      b. Reflecting group feelings
      c. Raising questions
      d. Calling attention to resources
      e. Sensitizing the group to better group work methods
         . . . will result in greater responsibility for the success of the group's activities. (Responsibility is defined as participating orally, making suggestions, making proposals for action, and voluntarily accepting responsibility for doing the job.)
   2. If (a) the agenda is planned cooperatively, (b) records of decisions are kept and progress is checked, and (c) individuals are encouraged to assume responsibilities, then the planning meetings will seem more worthwhile to the group members (Smith, 1952).
   Statements are often phrased as if/then hypotheses, or the more/the less and the higher/the lower. The improvement or action possibilities are described in the hypothesis itself.
C. COLLECTING THE EVIDENCE
   In this case, evidence was collected by interviewing at selected times during the semester, using questionnaires, and keeping records of what happened at meetings.
D. GENERALIZING
   The content was a great concern to these teachers. No one had been able to articulate the problem of what was wrong with the meetings, even as everyone was affected by them. This form of concurrent research and development involved people in taking action on their own problems and figuring out strategies for improvement. The group ended with the following generalizations (p. 60).
   1. The group assumed more responsibility when the leader limited her participation and helped the group become sensitive to theirs.
   2. The quantity *and* quality of responsibility increased.
   3. The use of written evaluation sheets helped develop the group's concerns about ways of working more effectively.
   4. Checking out what happened to the decisions was an important way of moving the group to carry through on its actions.
   5. These new skills affected other groups as the teachers learned how to work more effectively.
   6. Records of the meetings showed the growth of the group better than evaluation sheets.

What we see here is a process for solving problems in which teachers use as content their own problems and ideas for improving practices. Depending on the time, the problem, and the nature of the commitment, this melding of process and content could be carried on within the school;

if the problem is too serious, complicated, or needs an outside perspective, collaboration from a university or district person(s) could be sought, as in this example. Action research is a way of learning to better describe one's problems, and affords opportunities for actively engaging people in improving their own practices.

Interactive Research and Development on Teaching (IR&DT)

In the mid 1970s, Interactive Research and Development on Teaching (IR & DT) was conducted at two sites—one in San Diego, the other in Vermont (Tikunoff, Ward, and Griffin, 1975).

Several decades after the initial action research described by Corey, there is still a gap between those who do research on teachers and the reality of teaching. IR&DT attempts to provide an alternative to fill this gap. The purposes of this interactive stance are similar to earlier action research. A team of teachers, a developer, and a researcher work together to formulate a problem. They decide what evidence they need to collect, which is then used to intervene in a solution to the problem. In the San Diego team, the following transpired.

1. The teachers, developer, and researcher decided on a problem: How do teachers cope with distractions that keep them from providing more student time-on-task?

2. Teachers and the researcher observed during a three-month period using an observation checklist. Teachers kept logs of their distractions, and the ethnographer focused on the sequence of events and teacher-student interactions.

3. The findings revealed a complete description of distractions to classroom interactions including those generated by students (interrupting the teacher, making noise), those generated by the school (pull-out programs, clarifications of instruction), and irregularities such as unexpected visitors, speakers, and so forth.

4. Teachers used a variety of coping techniques to deal with the various kinds of distractions. Direct commands were most popular, but nonverbal actions (gestures, signs) were also prevalent.

5. Each teacher's distractions and techniques for coping were itemized and several selected as examples of more effective coping techniques; that is, the teachers intervened in their own classrooms to improve their coping techniques.

6. The teachers who were involved in this concurrent research and development then provided inservice education for the district.

Interactive Research and Development on Schooling (IR&DS)

Interactive Research and Development is an extension of Interactive Research. This new project focused on interactive research as an intervention strategy creating professional level development opportunities. The purposes of this project were to:

1. Conduct interactive research in three different settings.
2. Determine if professional growth was positive.
3. Determine whether the interactive strategy was appropriate for a variety of school issues.
4. Determine if the strategy could be conducted for a minimal amount of money.
5. Document the institutional contributions related to the success of the strategy.
6. Look carefully at the specific contexts to see if there were situation variables that related to how the strategy was implemented (Griffin and others, 1982).

Rather than studying the effects of the interactive strategy in one setting, the researchers decided to examine the strategy in several very different settings to determine the degree to which it contributed to the improvement of practice regardless of such issues as problem differences, context differences, organizational missions, and the like. In this project, three teams were organized, one each in (1) a suburban school district, (2) a teacher-union sponsored teacher center consortium, and (3) an intermediate agency whose mission is to provide services to several participating school districts. The central components of IR&DS included the following features:

1. The composition of the R&D teams was designed to ensure that the school practitioner role would be well represented.
2. The contribution of the role representatives on the R&D teams informed the R&D processes. (Practitioners used knowledge and skills related to schools and classrooms; researchers contributed to the research phase; and developers watched for school improvement activities.)
3. Responsibility was shared.
4. The strategy was problem focused. (That is, the problem under study had to be verified by the school members' colleagues.)
5. Research and development was concurrent or overlapping. (When the problem was developed for research, the team was already thinking about how the process or the results could be used for staff development.)

6. The actual research was conducted in schools while they were in session.

Three very different problems were researched by the teams. The school district studied the qualities of good writing in children; the teacher center specialist team studied the factors that enable teachers to maintain positive attitudes toward their jobs; and the Intermediate Agency studied several interventions designed to deal with reducing disruptive behavior in the classroom. At the end of the two years, the following observations were made.

- Participants believed they had learned a great deal about research and development. A dramatic outcome was that participants came to realize that development can be process oriented as well as product oriented.

- All team members developed some research skills and used them. Two of the teams, in particular, provided ample evidence of new skills in research *and* development.

- All three teams gained increased understanding of not only the problem they studied, but the complexity of making changes in their setting.

- All teams not only reported the impact the process had on them as individuals and team members, but on their school district environment as well.

- In two of the teams, the teachers played strong roles in the selection, design, data collection, analysis, and writing of the final report. In addition, these teacher teams were heavily involved in development for a larger group of teachers.

- We found that it was critical for the success of the team for the university researcher to have a strong and consistent commitment to "interactive" research and the possiblities and capabilities of teachers to engage in the research and development process.

- All three teams used the researcher as the primary souce of technical assistance, which bodes well for this team approach.

- Teachers reported heightened self-esteem based upon their newfound abilities to be involved with research.

This type of research *and* development makes provisions for dealing with several of our understandings.

- It breaks the isolation of teachers from one another and from others who might provide a supportive team.

- It recognizes and respects teachers' views of their problems.

- It puts teachers, researchers, and developers on a team where *all* can learn.
- It provides inservice activities for other teachers as it recognizes the classroom and school as legitimate contexts for research.
- Opportunities are created for trying out different roles.

Networks for School Improvement

We often think of solving problems in our own institutions. We rarely think of forming coalitions or networks *outside* existing formal channels. And it is even rarer that we think of these loose, informal collections of people (networks) as catalysts for change. We may very well be in a period where we grossly underestimate both the attack on teachers and the amount of support needed to make improvements in practice. Added to this, most of us grow up in formal organizations and do not think of providing informal settings and gatherings as legitimate strategies for improving and enhancing our knowledge. But we now have several good examples of such networks of people and more experience about their organization, focus, and effects (Miles, 1977; Sarason, 1977).

We discuss networks by describing several of them. Our concern is understanding them from the inside, getting a sense of the subleties, and using examples as a way of conceptualizing what we know about networks. We also begin to see the various forms networks can take as we look at a group of schools, a group of districts, and a nationwide group of innovators. The key ingredients described by Parker (1979) serve as an initial focus for our understanding. Those ingredients include a sense of being alternative, a sense of shared purpose, information sharing and psychological support, and voluntary and equal participation.

Behind these ingredients are an interesting array of nuances. For example, all school districts have inservice education. What would be so novel about a network that had school improvement as its focus? The network could be alternative in many ways: in its focus as the *Classroom Action Research Network**; in its values, activities, mechanism; or just by being more flexible or involving a different group of people.

---

*This network is international in scope and attempts to link teachers, researchers, and inservice educators who believe that "valid knowledge about classrooms depends on teachers being given, and accepting responsibility for generating that knowledge." (Cambridge Institute of Education, Shaftsbury Road, Cambridge, CB2, 2BX, England.)

The League of Cooperating Schools (LCS)

Many books have been written about the LCS. We refer the reader to them, for details, case histories, and important conceptual break-throughs about our understandings concerning the process of change (Goodlad, 1975; Bentzen, 1974; Williams, 1974). What we intend here is to discuss specifically the building of networks as a way of providing school improvement.

The League was a collaboration of 18 schools. Districts were members but those who attended meetings were primarily the teachers and principals at the 18 schools. Also involved in the network was the /I/D/E/A/staff. The major linkage took place between a small staff known as SECSI (Study of Educational Change and School Improvement) and 18 principals and many of the teachers from the schools.

The overarching focus of this network was to understand the nature of change and to effect school improvement. These purposes were sufficiently compelling to involve people and sufficiently ambiguous to keep dialog going for years. This is an important point! A focus that is too narrow can't sustain, yet one that is too broad may involve people in activities not easily related to the main focus. The challenge is to collectively provide for a focus that engages people in activities of sufficient interest and involvement, and to be sensitive to the changes in development as the network grows older and more sophisticated. That is no easy task, but this fact is what makes a network attractive. And it is this characteristic that makes a network different from the formal organization of its members.

In the League, researchers and school people came together. In the beginning there was much discomfort as the researchers struggled with measurement problems and descriptions of dynamic processes that wouldn't lend themselves to neat, tidy categories. School people, on the other hand, wanted answers to their problems—not questionnaires. But it was precisely the mix of these two disparate groups that made this network grow in its understandings of schools as each group became more tolerant, less afraid to expose what they didn't know, and more open to finding out what could be learned from collective struggle.

Much information was shared in the League, but it changed in both substance and form. Initially, it came from the top—from "experts" in the field. But it was whittled, reworked, recreated, and translated by teachers and principals. The concepts were from the experts but the teachers were the "experts" in making it work in the classroom. (Much of the focus for school improvement during the LCS involved individualizing instruction.)

Activities began at a posh local hotel with a formal luncheon and ended five years later at a school with a sack lunch. Publications went from slick professionally printed newsletters to dittoed teacher materials—a tribute not to declining funds, but to the growing importance of content over form.

There was always a core group of people who came to meetings. But from time to time people drifted in and out on a voluntary basis. This point too makes networks of an entirely different order than formal groups. No one is checking up. No one is taking attendance. One belongs because one wants to attend. Clearly information was being shared in the League, and people felt as if they were among friends who were learning to respect differences. Who decides the substance for the meetings? Who participates as learner, leader, creator? Those questions changed over time. The "experts" learned the limits of their expertise. All of us were experts at one time or another. It is these changing norms and the possibilities for establishing new ones that differentiate these loose arrangements from more formal organizations.

The National Diffusion Network (NDN)

The NDN is a federally sponsored approach to spreading exemplary programs (Neill, 1980), which range from basic skills to special education to career education. (For a complete description of programs, see *Education Programs that Work,* 1980). They also represent a variety of philosophical and psychological perspectives (Pasch, 1981). NDN is a different kind of network in that the content of many of the programs being disseminated has been created by teachers in concert with others to solve their own teaching problems. In order to share their programs, they must provide evidence that the program has improved skills, attitudes, or behaviors of pupils. Approval is given by applying to the Joint Dissemination Review Panel. Upon approval, dissemination funds are given to state facilitators who in turn can make these programs available to schools in the states.

NDN's members have over a decade of experience in implementing school improvement programs that appear to be successful (Crandall, 1983). In studying 61 different innovative practices in over 400 classrooms in ten states, it was found that many of the programs, although implemented several years earlier, are still in place. Factors that contributed to the success of these programs include:

- Commitment of teachers in using the new practice
- Carefully developed curricular and instructional practices
- Training by credible people
- Assistance and support from other teachers, principals, district staff, and external people
- Attention to such factors as line items on budgets, writing new programs into curriculum guides (Loucks, 1983).

If we go back to Parker's key ingredients, we get a better sense of how NDN works and how networks can provide the glue for school improvement activities. NDN is clearly an alternative to the formal modes of delivering inservice education in that ideas (programs) are created from the "bottom up," and packaged and sold by the creators themselves. But the significance lies in the fact that the creation *starts* with the teacher. Furthermore, for the most part, developer/demonstrators have been teachers or have taken part in developing the programs and learning how to provide for teacher learning. They know they must establish credibility among teachers.

NDNers all care about school improvement even though their definition of what this looks like varies with the program. NDN meetings are characterized by information sharing, not only on programs, but on "strands" (such as leadership, evaluation, and so forth) that represent important thrusts for all the membership. But clearly over the years there have been much support and sharing of people who have learned by doing; how to get ideas into a teacher's classroom, how to provide the practical help necessary to make it stick while at the same time learning the needs of what NDNers themselves need to stay alive.

The Metropolitan School Study Council (MSSC)

MSSC is a tri-state network including New York, New Jersey, and Connecticut linking 29 school districts and Teachers College, Columbia University. It was founded in 1941 by Paul Mort, an administration professor at Teachers College.

During the last six years it has shifted direction from a study council to a focus on school improvement and a growing awareness of the utility of sharing resources. Earlier in its existence, MSSC served as a vehicle for research on schools and providing schools with the latest research or theory on educational practices. This is still a legitimate function, but it has been expanded to consciously link information in the university with people in the field. And the *form* and *substance* are different. Work groups that encourage informal dialog in a neutral setting are different from inservice in the district or classes in the university. Subnetworks have been created by facilitating groups of districts where there are common concerns (such as a writing consortium and a new computer group). Where did we ever get the idea that a teacher, school, district, or university could go it alone or that any of us alone had to be all-knowing?

This network has continued to shift its focus as members' needs shift. The university is concerned with research and its relations to the field, but the school people are concerned with knowledge that is practical and sensitive to their shifting pressures. Rewards for university professors are in publications and research—for school people they are in raising achievement scores, teaching children how to read and think critically. The pursuit of cooperation between these kinds of demands is what makes the creation and maintenance of a network both problematic and possible.

Organizing a Network

Good will or the announcement of a new network is not enough to *organize* a network. One must also determine how the network is to function. We offer eight processes that we consider essential for the creation of a network (Lieberman, 1977). They come from our participation in and reflection on what makes the loose, informal nature of a network compelling to its members.

- *Organizing for participation.* A group of people, including key decision makers, need to be involved in the formation.
- *Developmental substance* (such as content around questions of personal concern and local problems) should be the basis for starting a network. It will change as the needs of the participants change.
- *Developmental mechanisms,* including meetings, groups, workshops, consortia. While speeches and "telling" usually inspire the formation of a network, they are later replaced by more interaction and more shared decisions and shared leadership.
- *Planning new rewards,* which includes paying attention to time, meeting people, refreshments, as well as providing for more cosmopolitan experiences and experimenting with new ideas.
- *Problem-solving orientation.* In order to open people to new ideas, help them adapt to changing conditions, or deliberately change one's

own work, the network needs to develop its members' capacity to solve their own problems.

• *Diagnosis.* This includes finding out what people know, what they need, and what pressures they're under. This is a continuous process that helps the network adapt to changing times, needs, and learnings of its members.

• *Strategy building.* This is the process of creating action plans and includes ways of moving the group and dealing with conflicts, tensions, and complexities—all of which make networks alternative.

• *Organizing for linkage.* This is the process of joining different people together who agree on the large goals (school improvement), but who have different reasons for participating, different perspectives, or different contributions to make.

Districtwide School Improvement

There are many ways in which school districts first become involved with school improvement efforts. Sometimes they are initiated by a district staff developer; in many cases it is the job of the assistant superintendent for instruction to organize school improvement efforts. The extent to which these individuals are supported has much to do with the seriousness with which boards of education and their superintendents take the whole matter of professional development.

The following example is based on what happened in a medium-sized, urban school district when teachers became involved in districtwide improvements and their own professional development.

A Districtwide Approach

An unmet need in our district was the availability of remedial materials in language arts and reading, which elementary teachers could use as part of their regular classroom instruction. Our Chapter One program provided a pull-out approach. Teachers wanted to complement this with a strategy that could be easily incorporated into the regular classroom.

After studying a variety of possibilities, a group of principals and teachers approached me, the Assistant Superintendent of Curriculum, and asked for support for a project that would involve teachers in materials development. The materials would be keyed to district learning objectives, to the local competency tests, to standardized tests, and to the newly adopted reading program. As a result, teachers would be able to assess student needs using a variety of instru-

ments, and to provide on-the-spot remediation as soon as deficiencies were uncovered.

With the enthusiastic backing of the board of education, we decided to hire teachers for two weeks during the summer to develop the materials. Over 45 teachers participated. Under the direction of our Reading and Language Arts Coordinator, the teachers were organized into grade-level committees. Each committee was to develop three to five direct teaching lessons for approximately 20 objectives at each grade. The teachers worked in groups in their living rooms, basements, and attics across the district. A steering committee, composed of one representative from each grade-level committee, was organized and met twice a week. The steering committee reviewed and monitored all materials that were developed.

By the end of the summer, teachers had developed an enormous quantity of materials. Thanks to the efforts of the district print shop, all materials were printed and collected by the first week of school. Personnel in the curriculum office prepared separate "buckets" for each grade level. Each bucket contained a series of lessons, grouped by objectives and files in manila folders. The complete buckets were available to all participating teachings for use in their individual classrooms. In addition, three principals and their staffs volunteered to pilot the materials on a schoolwide basis.

Each of the three pilot schools approached the implementation process differently. Complete control for implementation was placed in the hands of the teachers and principals in the schools. Each school selected a steering committee of teachers who oversaw the process. The steering committee monitored teacher use of the materials, assessed needs in the building, and developed their own staff development programs. The district level curriculum staff served as consultants to the schools on an invitational basis. That is, the district staff responded to expressed staff needs rather than taking a leadership position. Among the results of this approach was the development of a microcomputer management system, which helped teachers correlate the remedial materials to student achievement data. In addition, specially tailored inservice sessions were held at each school, and classroom assistance was provided on an individual basis.

At this writing, we are in the sixth month of our pilot project. At the end of the school year, the teachers who used the materials will meet with the central office staff to assess the quality of the materials, to refine and revise them, and to plan for districtwide implementation of the program. We are very pleased with our success so far and have become reaffirmed in our belief that districtwide improvement takes place under the same supportive conditions that are effective in building-level projects.

Teacher-Run Professional Development Efforts

Sometimes professional development can be initiated and sustained by teachers running their own improvement efforts. We describe two such efforts: a teacher institute run in a district, and a series of teacher centers led by teacher specialists who are paid on a teacher line.

The Teacher Institute

In this instance, a teacher from the high school is released half time to administer an institute that provides for a variety of staff development opportunities run by teachers for teachers. The person who administers the program also works half time as an English teacher. In this way a district not only has an internal staff developer, but the institute can be sensitive to teacher needs, as well as district concerns. Such inservice activities include environmental studies, interdisciplinary studies, film and ideology, computer uses, stress among adolescents, strategies for helping. Teachers from the district teach other teachers a variety of subject and content areas. The track record of this kind of arrangement can be quite strong in that teachers pick up other tips from teachers. The teachers are respected because they are currently teaching and the content of their workshops is "not theoretical" but tried in the classroom. By providing teachers the leadership, the teacher's view of district concerns becomes the dominant mode, rather than what the teacher must do to meet district requirements. The difference is subtle, yet important: in this case, the head of the Teacher Institute is chosen by the teacher organization, which means that the teachers' own organization is in charge and held accountable for teachers' professional development. There is also an accreditation board made up of teachers and administrators who recommend courses to the board of education for approval and salary credit. In this way the district has a stake in the institute as well. This arrangement does not mean that the arrangements must be adversarial. Effective teacher-run staff development can be a significant complement to other administrative school improvement concerns. But both the administration and the teacher organization must be able to communicate their similar and different concerns and have some means to negotiate these (Schwartz, 1982).

The Teacher Center

In the past decade there have been several different models of what has come to be known as the teacher center. In this form of teacher-run professional development, an actual room is run by and for teachers for the express purpose of providing professional growth incentives for teachers. In New York City, for example, there are several teacher centers in both elementary and high schools that are maintained by teacher specialists associated with the United Federation of Teachers (UFT). These people have been chosen by extensive interview techniques, paid on a teacher line, and trained to provide a variety of services for teachers (Leiter and Cooper, 1978).

Any school can find some room or place where materials can be collected and workshops held, and where teachers can come to get help, develop materials, or converse with fellow teachers. The site is important because it represents a place for people to come and talk, get help and support, be exposed to new ideas, and even relax with a cup of coffee.

The role of the teacher specialist is varied and complex. In some instances it is to introduce people to a variety of effective teaching ideas and to know how to be sensitive to teacher wants or needs. It is also to motivate people to try new techniques or understand new tools or new regulations. A center can also be a place where teachers can legitimately teach their fellow teachers the best of what they have learned. In other cases, the actual place for the center can become a focus for professional talk, lectures, shared dialog, or more formal sessions on a new technique supported by the school but learned in the center. (Teachers may create mastery learning materials in an attempt to learn about the concepts of mastery. Or, as we have observed, the center can provide for training about computers.) The discussion about Master Teachers has already been pre-empted by roles such as these that have already been created. The importance of this mode of professional development cannot be overestimated. At its best, a teacher center run by a teacher specialist can provide sensitive, peer-oriented, practical assistance by teachers who gain the respect of other teachers by their expertise in teaching, their sensitivity to the craft of teaching, and their understanding of the vulnerability and defensiveness of teachers, which can be overcome by working to help teachers help themselves. A nonevaluative, supportive, and humane environment where teachers can come without fear of exposure can be a powerful place to learn. In addition, on-site centers run by specialists can provide demonstrations in class, provide immediate help and feedback, and be counted on by teachers to give quality help in a teacher-oriented way.

In the teacher institute, teachers come voluntarily and pay for a course/seminar/workshop format after school. Because the center is on-site, before school, lunch, prep periods as well as in-class time can be utilized.

Learning from Research, Craft, and Intuition

We have come full circle in our discussion. We began with a description of the social realities of teachers, looking inside to see how teachers think and carry out their work in elementary and secondary schools. We then looked at studies of school improvement efforts to unwrap the complexities of the social system of schools. Lastly, we described a variety of ways to organize and carry out school improvement efforts. In closing, we want to resist the temptation to "wrap it all up" and present formulae for successful school change. What we can do, by way of summary, is to array some of the learnings we have gathered from the research, from a conscious understanding of practice, and from active participation in and thinking about school improvement and staff development. Such an array of learnings would include:

- Working *with* people rather than working *on* them.
- Recognizing the complexity and craft nature of the teacher's work.
- Understanding that there are unique cultural differences in each school. These effect both where school improvement efforts begin and what form they will take.
- Providing time to learn for adults. The more people work with each other, the more energy and skills they need and the more people will see each other as colleagues.
- Building collaboration and cooperation involves the provision for people doing things together, talking together, sharing concerns. Over time, this helps build group norms.
- Starting where the people are, not where you are.
- Caring for people first and techniques second.
- Making private knowledge public by being sensitive to the effects of isolation and trial-and-error learning on teachers.
- Resisting simplistic solutions to complex problems. Getting comfortable with reworking, finding enhanced understanding and enlightenment.
- Appreciating that there are many variations of school and professional development efforts. There is no one way.

• Using knowledge as a mode of helping people grow rather than pointing to their deficits.

• Supporting improvement efforts by protecting ideas, providing time, announcing expectations, making provisions for the necessary resources.

• Sharing leadership functions with a team so that people can provide complementary skills and get experience in role taking.

• Organizing school improvement activities around a particular focus.

• Understanding that successful improvement efforts have content that is salient but must also have a process or a structure to go with it.

• Being sensitive to and aware of the differences between the worlds of the teacher and the principal. They share a part of their work—time, climate of the school, and the possibility for group cohesion—but there are demands on each that they do not share, which cause a natural and problematic relationship. Collaborative efforts mediate this relationship.

We know that this list is not complete. We look forward to adding to it as our own experience and knowledge, and that of others engaged in the task of improving schools, increase.

Figure 5. Adult Development as a Source of Content

Source	Major Focus
Stages of Teacher Development (Field, 1979).	Field, a 4th grade teacher herself, interviewed teachers and grouped their responses into three identifiable stages, which relate to teachers' handling of the following activities:

1. Arranging the classroom
2. Planning the day
3. Planning large groups
4. Diagnosis
5. Record keeping
6. Parent conferences
7. Unstructured time
8. Transitions
9. Student behavior
10. Self-concept/self-evaluation

Stage One. Concern with day-to-day survival; use of hit-or-miss strategies. Teachers feel inadequate to deal with the complexities of the classroom. The children, materials, physical environment, subjects, and self are all seen as separate entities.

Stage Two. Increased self-confidence based on successes with students. Teachers speak about some appropriate solutions to problems. They can now plan for a few weeks rather than day-by-day.

Stage Three. Teachers can see the classroom as a whole and everything as a potential resource to be used. Physical and social environment are all tools to create a rich learning environment. Flexibility, openness, experimentation are all part of the repertoire.

Source	Major Focus
Beyond Surface Curriculum (Bussis, Chittenden, and Amarel, 1976).	This research team interviewed 60 elementary teachers attempting to implement "more informal approaches to instruction." All of the teachers were receiving some kind of help from advisors. Two sets of priorities were inferred from the teacher interviews. Within each priority, teachers were identified as having narrow, middle-range, and comprehensive concerns.

	Cognitive Priorities	*Personal/Social Priorities*
Narrow	Major concern about the basics. Grade level facts and skills.	Concern about good school behavior/ docility; politeness, working hard, settling down predominate.
Mid-Range	Initiative/independence; assume responsibility for own learning. Become self-directed.	Confidence/commitment; concern that children feel good about themselves. Stops at children being happy.
Comprehensive	Reflectivity/intention; concern that children know "what they are about and	Awareness/acceptance of self; deeper concern that students can differentiate

why." *Their purposes are included.*

feelings and abilities. Major concern that students know themselves in their own terms.

Conceptual Systems and Personality Organization (Harvey, Hunt, and Shroder, 1961).

Conceptual development is characterized by the interaction of one's personality with the environment. Four stages are described:

First Stage: Unilateral Dependence. Characterized by submissiveness to external control—the classical "Tell me what to do" syndrome. Thinking is concrete. In a typical school situation, teachers ask the consultant, principal, or another to give them direction or tell them what it all means.

Second Stage: Negative Independence. A resistant stage; the "budding of internal control," characterized by a fair amount of conflict. People are less predictable and dependable and therefore often more threatening because they are harder to control.

Third Stage: Conditional Dependence and Mutuality. A more objective view of the social environment; a less subjective stage. One entertains alternative views of self and events. Cooperation rather than submission evolving; power problem is resolved. Healing wounds and maintaining harmony are important.

Fourth Stage: Positive Independence. It is here that group members accept one another. If there is conflict, it is over substance. Consensus is reached based on rational decisions over tasks.

Figure 6. Concepts of Adult Development

Source	Major Concepts
"Personalizing Staff Development" in *Staff Development: New Demands, New Realities, New Perspectives* (Hall and Loucks, 1979).	These authors have developed a profile of concerns that teachers have as they deal with innovations. Although they do not occur one at a time, they appear to have levels of intensity and follow a development path. There are seven stages of concern about an innovation:* 0 Little concern about or involvement with the innovation. 1 *Informational.* Interest in learning more. Interest in substance of the innovation is unrelated to self. 2 *Personal.* Interest in one's own adequacy to meet the demands of the innovation. 3 *Management.* Interest in how one organizes, schedules, and uses the innovation. 4 *Consequence.* Focus on the impact of the innovation on students. 5 *Collaboration.* Focus on cooperating with others. 6 *Refocusing.* Focus on larger benefits or more powerful alternatives to innovation. These stages of concern are useful in thinking about still another form of developmental sequence; in this case, the stages of concern as they relate to a new idea. *Based on original concept of Hall, Wallace, and Dossett (1973).
Humanizing Schools: New Directions, New Decisions, Maturity and Competence: A Transcultural View (Heath, 1977).	There are principles of maturation that can be applied to teacher growth: 1. *Enhancing symbolization:* (a) providing challenge; (b) teaching about reflection upon one's own growth. 2. *Furthering multiple perspectives:* (a) creating a climate of trust; (b) providing for people to take other roles; (c) expecting people to be responsible for other's growth (mutual obligation). 3. *Increasing integration:* (a) encouraging active involvement; (b) providing experiential learning; (c) modeling integration of different ways of thinking. 4. *Helping stabilize growth:* (a) allow person to experience consequences of decisions and acts; (b) appreciate and affirm strengths. 5. *Make learning autonomous:* (a) encourage responsibility for person's own growth; (b) test and apply learning in varied situations; (c) provide test for person's autonomy.
Value Development as the Aim of Education (Sprinthall and Mosher, 1978).	Using Dewey, Piaget, Loevinger, and Kohlberg, the authors describe adult development based on four concepts: (1) role taking—try new interpersonal tasks; (2) reflection—think about and learn from experience; (3) challenge; and (4) support.

References

Barnes, S. *Synthesis of Selected Research on Teaching Findings.* Austin: Research and Development Center for Teacher Education, University of Texas, 1981.

Bentzen, Mary M. *Changing Schools: The Magic Feather Principle.* New York: McGraw Hill, 1974.

Biles, Brenda; Billups, L.; and Veitch, S. *Educational Research and Dissemination Program—Training and Resource Manual.* Washington, D.C.: American Federation of Teachers, 1983.

Bussis, Anne M.; Chittenden, Edward A.; and Amarel, Marianne. *Beyond Surface Curriculum: An Interview Study of Teacher Understandings.* Boulder, Colo.: Westview Press, 1976.

Corey, Stephen. *Action Research to Improve School Practices.* New York: Teachers College, Columbia University, 1953.

Crandall, David, and associates. "People, Policies and Practices: Examining the Chain of School Improvement." Andover, Mass.: The Network, 1983.

Culver, Carman M., and Hoban, Gary A., eds. *The Power to Change: Issues for the Innovator Educator.* New York: McGraw Hill, 1973.

Education Programs That Work. 7th ed. San Francisco: Far West Laboratory, 1980.

Edward, S. *Changing Teacher Practice: A Synthesis of Relevant Research.* Austin: Research and Development Center for Teacher Education, The University of Texas, 1981.

Field, Kristin. *Teacher Development: A Study of the Stages in Development of Teachers.* Brookline, Mass.: Teacher Center, 1979.

Gibson, Tony. *Teachers Talking: Aims, Methods, Attitudes to Change:* London: Allen Lane, 1973.

Goodlad, John I. *The Dynamics of Educational Change.* New York: McGraw Hill, 1975.

Greene, Maxine. *The Teacher as Stranger—Educational Philosophy for the Modern Age.* Belmont, Calif.: Wadsworth Publishing, 1973.

Griffin, G., and others. "Changing Teacher Practice. Final Report of an Experimental Study." Austin: Research and Development Center for Teacher Education, University of Texas, 1983.

Griffin, E.; Lieberman, A.; and Noto, J.J. "Interactive Research and Development on Schooling, Final Report of the Implementation of the Strategy." New York: Teachers College, Columbia University, 1982.

Hall, G.E.; Wallace, R.C., Jr.; and Dossett, W.A. *A Developmental Conceptualization of the Adoption Process Within Educational Institutions.* Austin: Research and Development Center for Teacher Education, The University of Texas, 1973.

Hall, Gene, and Loucks, Susan M. "Personalizing Staff Development." In *Staff Development: New Demands, New Realities, New Perspectives.* New York: Teachers College Press, 1979.

Harvey, O.J.; Hunt, David E.; and Shroder, Harold. *Conceptual Systems and Personality Organization.* New York: John Wiley and Sons, 1961.

Heath, Douglas. *Humanizing Schools: New Directions, New Decisions. Maturity and Competence: A Transcultural View.* New York: Wiley and Sons (Gardner), 1977.

Huff, Ann. "Planning to Plan." In *New Perspectives on Planning in Educational Organizations*. Edited by David Clark. San Francisco: Far West Laboratory, 1981.

Interactive Research and Development on Schooling Newsletter #1. Horace Mann-Lincoln Institute. New York: Teachers College, Columbia University, 1981.

Kepler, Karen B. "Potentials and Limitations of Policy for Improving Education." In *Complexities of Policy Making in Education*. Edited by A. Lieberman and M. McLaughlin. Chicago: University of Chicago Press, 1982.

Kounin, Jacob. *Discipline and Group Management in Classrooms*. New York: Holt, Rinehart & Winston, 1970.

Lieberman, Ann. "Linking Processes in Educational Change." In *Linking Processes in Educational Improvement*. Edited by N. Nash and J. Culbertson. Columbus, Ohio: Council on Educational Administration.

Leiter, Maurice, and Cooper, Myrna. "How Teacher Unionists View In-Service Education." *Teachers College Record* 80, 1 (September 1978).

Little, Judith W. *School Success and Staff Development: The Role of Staff Development in Urban Desegregated Schools*. Boulder, Colo.: Center for Action Research, Inc., 1981.

Loucks, Susan. "At Last: Some Good News from a Study of School Improvement." *Educational Leadership* 41, 3 (November 1983): 4–5.

Miles, Matthew. "Networking." New York: Center for Policy Research, June 1977.

Neill, Shirley Boes. "Spreading the Word: The National Diffusion Network." *National Elementary Principal* (June 1980): 45–48.

Neill, Shirley Boes. "Teachers Hit the Road." *American Education* (May 1980): 16–19.

Oja, Sharon, and Sprinthall, Norman A. "Psychological and Moral Development for Teachers: Can You Teach Old Dogs?" In *Value Development as the Aim of Education*. Edited by N. Sprinthall and R. Mosher. Schenectady, N.Y.: Character Research Press, 1978.

Parker, L. Allen. "Networks for Innovation and Problem Solving and Their Use for Improving Education: A Comparative Review." Washington, D.C.: Dissemination Processes Seminar IV, October 1979.

Pasch, Marvin. "Using the Developer-Demonstrators of the National Diffusion Network to Expand Higher Education's Professional Development Capacity." Paper presented before the Eastern Educational Research Association, Philadelphia, March 1981.

Sarason, Seymour; Carroll, C.; Maton, K.; Cohen, S.; and Lorenz, E. *Resources, Community and Exchange Networks*. San Francisco: Jossey-Bass, 1977.

Schon, Donald. "Coping Networks." Boston: Massachusetts Institute of Technology, unpublished paper.

Schwartz, Judith. "Scarsdale Teacher Institute: A Model of Teacher Directed In-Service." Paper delivered before the Association for Supervision and Curriculum Development, March 1982.

Smith, Mary Neel. In *The School Review* 60 (March 1952): 142–150.

Smyth, W. John. "Research on Classroom Management: Studies of Pupil Engaged Learning Time as a Special But Instructive Case." Prepared for the *British*

Journal of Teacher Education, Deakin University, 1980.

Sprinthall, Norman, and Mosher, Ralph L., eds. *Value Development as the Aim of Education.* Schenectady, N.Y.: Character Research Press, 1978.

Stallings, Jane. "Changing Teacher Behavior: A Challenge for the Eighties." Paper delivered at the American Educational Research Association, Los Angeles, 1981.

Tikunoff, William; Ward, Beatrice A.; and Griffin, Gary A. *Interactive Research and Development on Teaching Study, Final Report.* San Francisco: Far West Laboratory, 1975.

Waller, Willard. *The Sociology of Teaching.* New York: John Wiley & Sons, 1967.

Williams, Richard C.; Wall, Charles; Martin, W. Michael; and Berchin, Arthur. *Effecting Organizational Renewal in Schools.* New York: McGraw Hill, 1974.

Index

Didactic approach to teaching, 44
Differentiated staffing, 85, 97
Discovery method, 113–114
Dossett, W. A., 142
Dreeben, Robert, 90, 100, 102

Edmonds, Ron, 89, 101
Educational reform. *See* School improvement
Educational Research and Dissemination Program (ER&D), 123–124
Edward, S., 122
Effective schools research, 89–90
Elementary schools, 17–36; case studies of, 18–24, 31–34; dilemmas of teachers in, 20–21, 82, 84, 102; first day of school year in, 18–24; principals of, 27–31; rhythms of teaching in, 6, 18–24; school improvement and, 24–34; teacher–student interaction in, 10–11
Elmore, Richard, 100
Emrich, John, 87, 91, 99, 100, 103
Engagement for teachers, 118–120

Faculty culture, 47–50, 53, 83–84
Farrar, Eleanor, 103
Feelings, 2, 13–14, 15
Feitler, Fred, 101
Field, Kristin, 94, 110, 111, 140
Florio, D., 103
Fullan, Michael, 103

Geoffrey, William, 21
Giacquinta, Joseph, 25*n*, 87, 92, 96, 100, 103
Gibbon, Peter, 30
Gibson, Troy, 84, 87, 98, 102, 114
Goals, of education, 3
Gold, Barry, 92, 103
Goldberg, Jo Ann, 85, 99
Goodlad, John I., 84, 89, 96, 100, 103, 130
Grace, Gerald, 84, 97, 100, 102
Greene, Maxine, 110
Griffin, E., 121, 127
Griffin, Gary A., 126
Griffiths, Daniel E., 105
Gross, Neal, 25*n*, 70, 87, 96, 100, 103

Hall, Gene E., 103, 111, 142
Harvey, O. J., 111, 141
Havelock, Ronald, 103
Heath, Douglas, 111, 142
Herriott, Robert, 70
High schools. *See* Secondary schools

Hoban, G., 96
House, Ernest, 92
Huberman, A., 85, 99
Huff, Ann, 124
Hunt, David E., 111, 141

Idealism, of new teachers, 7–8
Identification, faculty culture and, 48–49
Individually Guided Education (IGE), 85–86
Interactions: in faculty culture of secondary schools, 47–50, 53; feelings in, 13–14, 15; teacher–principal, 12, 27–29, 54–55; among teachers, 8–9, 11, 13–14, 29–31, 47–50, 53, 55–56; of teachers and students, 9–11
Interactive Research and Development on Schooling (IR&DS), 127–129
Interactive Research and Development on Teaching (IR&DT), 126
Interpersonal relations. *See* Interactions
Isolation: of principals, 71–72; of teachers, 4, 9, 13–14, 47–50, 86, 90–91

Jackson, Philip, 30, 90

Kahn, Robert L., 90
Katz, Daniel, 90
Keith, Pat, 25*n*, 83, 87, 96, 103
Kepler, Karen B., 22, 102, 113
Knowledge base, of teaching, 3, 7–9
Kounin, Jacob, 119

League of Cooperating Schools (LCS), 86–87, 96, 130–131
Leiter, Maurice, 27, 137
Lewin, Kurt, 91, 103
Lezotte, Lawrence W., 26, 89, 101
Lieberman, Ann, 17–18, 26, 28, 29, 100, 103, 133
Lightfoot, Sara Lawrence, 37
Lipham, James, 100
Little, Judith W., 120, 121, ₁23
Local problem solving, 114–115
Loneliness, of teachers, 4, 9, 13–14, 47–50, 86, 90–91
Lortie, Dan C., 2, 7, 20, 30, 44, 49, 80, 90, 100, 102
Lotto, Linda, 101
Loucks, Susan M., 103, 111, 132, 142

Maiocco, Donald, 100
Marsh, D., 27

148

Mastery learning, 30, 120–121, 137
McCarthy, M., 101
McLaughlin, Milbrey, 27, 29, 61, 73, 77, 86, 91, 98, 100, 101, 103
McPherson, Gertrude, 9, 25n, 86, 98, 100, 102
Metropolitan School Study Council (MSSC), 132–133
Meyer, John, 28, 101
Miles, M., 92, 103
Miles, Matthew B., 89, 100, 129
Miles, Michael, 85, 99
Miller, Lynne, 28, 41, 62–70
Mission, of teachers, 2, 46–47, 53
Moral authority, of principals, 76–77
Mort, Paul, 132
Mosher, Ralph L., 111, 142

National Diffusion Network (NDN), 131–132
Neill, Shirley Boes, 131
Networks: League of Cooperating Schools (LCS), 86–87, 96, 130–131; Metropolitan School Study Council (MSSC), 132–133; National Diffusion Network (NDN), 131–132; organizing, 133–134; for school improvement, 129–134
Norms: faculty culture and, 48–49; need for teaching, 3–4, 14; school culture and, 83–85, 93–94, 100–101

Observation, 9
Oja, Sharon, 112
Order. See Control

Parker, L. Allen, 129, 132
Pasch, Marvin, 131
Peer group, faculty culture as, 48–50
Peltzman, Barbara, 22
Peterson, Susan, 87, 91, 99, 100, 103
Planning, of school improvement, 59, 88
Popkewitz, Thomas, 85, 99
Power. See Authority; Control
Practical knowledge, 7–9, 78
Principals, 61–80; elementary school, 27–31; roles of, 70–77; school improvement and, 24, 54–55, 77–80; secondary school, 38, 54–55, 62–70; teacher interaction with, 12, 27–29, 54–55; weekly rhythms and, 62–70, 72
Privacy rule, 8–9, 13–14, 71–72
Problem solving: action research in, 124–

126; local, 114–115; networks and, 133–134
Purkey, Stewart C., 90

Rand Change Agent Study, 86–87
Record keeping: by principals, 73–74; by secondary school teachers, 41
Referee, principal as, 72–73
Reform. See School improvement
Research and Development Center for Teacher Education, 121–123
Reutter, Michael, 89, 97, 100, 101, 103
Rewards: faculty culture as source of, 48–49; from students, 2, 11
Rhythms, 5–7, 14; elementary school, 6, 18–24; principals and, 62–70, 72; secondary school, 6, 40–43, 52
Rules, 15; control and, 3–4, 14; faculty culture, 48–49; privacy, 8–9, 13–14, 71–72; school culture and, 83–85, 93–94, 100–101; of teaching, 7–9

Sarason, Seymour B., 4, 17, 20, 25–26, 73, 75, 81, 83, 96, 100, 129
Schlecty, Phillip C., 100
School culture, 83–85, 93–94, 100–101
School districts, and school improvement, 134–135
School improvement: awareness activities in, 112–113; case studies of, 31–34, 56–59, 96–99; concurrent research and development in, 124–129; conditions leading to, 86–87; development of teachers in, 110–142; districtwide, 134–135; effective schools research and, 89–90; elementary school, 24–34; faculty culture and, 83–84; implementation of, 93, 103; interactions among teachers and, 27–31, 54–56; isolation and, 86, 90–91; linear paths vs. detours in, 85–86; nature of schools and, 100–101; networks in, 129–134; participation in, 92–93, 103; planning for, 59, 88; political nature of change and, 92; principals and, 24, 54–55, 77–80; process of, 103; school culture and, 83–85, 93–94, 100–101; secondary school, 50–59; self-analysis by teachers and, 113–124; social context of teaching and, 24–25, 50–52; stages of, 91, 103, 110–111; strategies for organizing, 112–138; substance of education and, 26–27, 53–54; teacher characteristics and, 25–26, 52–53, 102; teacher-run efforts in, 136–138; teachers as adult learners in,

149

ABOUT THE AUTHORS

Ann Lieberman is a professor in the Department of Curriculum and Teaching at Teachers College, Columbia University, and co-director of the National Center for Restructuring Education, Schools and Teaching (NCREST). She has recently been named president of the American Educational Research Association (AERA).

Lynne Miller is a professor of education and executive director of the Southern Maine Partnership (a school/university collaboration) at the University of Southern Maine, where she also directs teacher education.